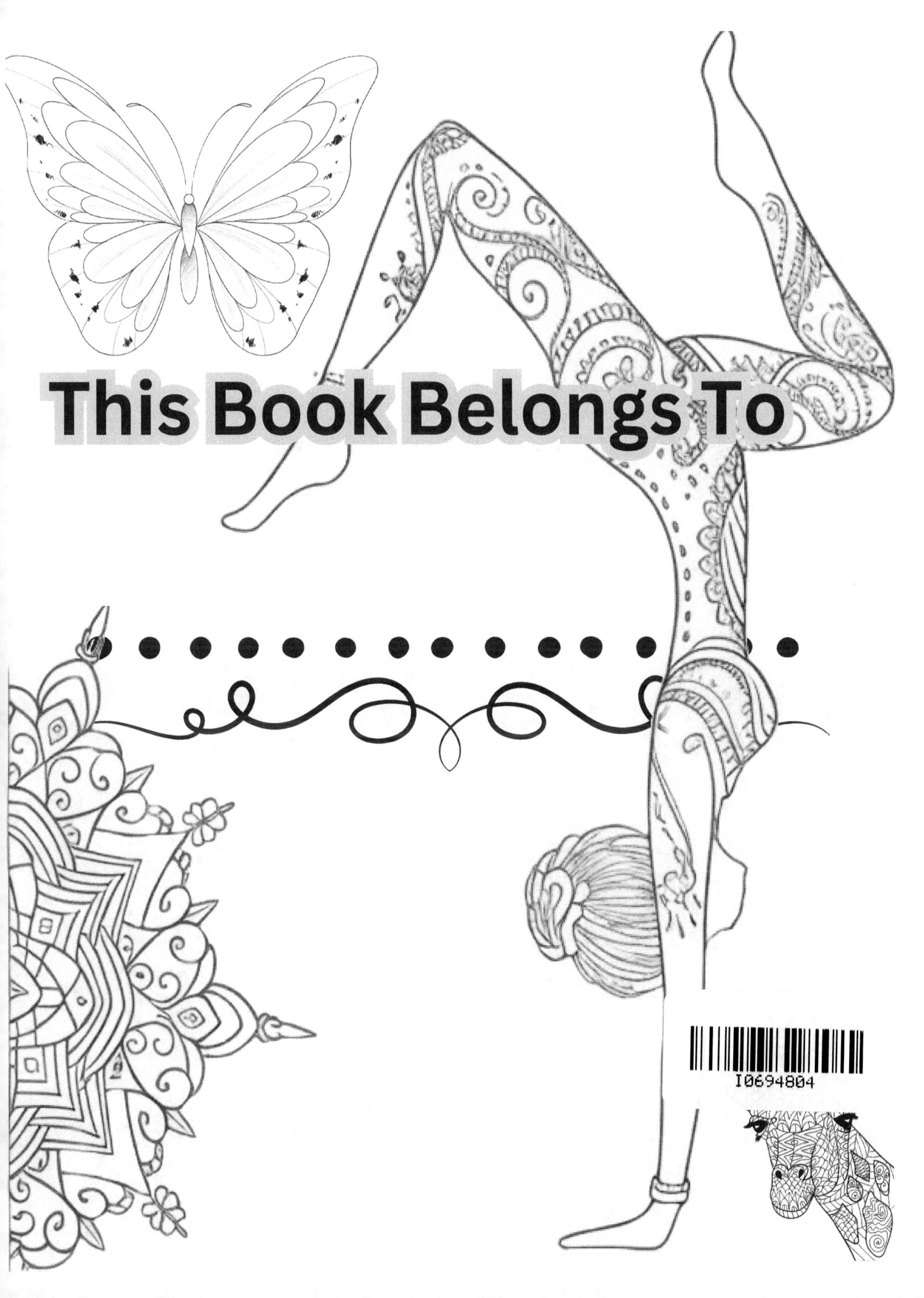
This Book Belongs To
. . . .
I0694804

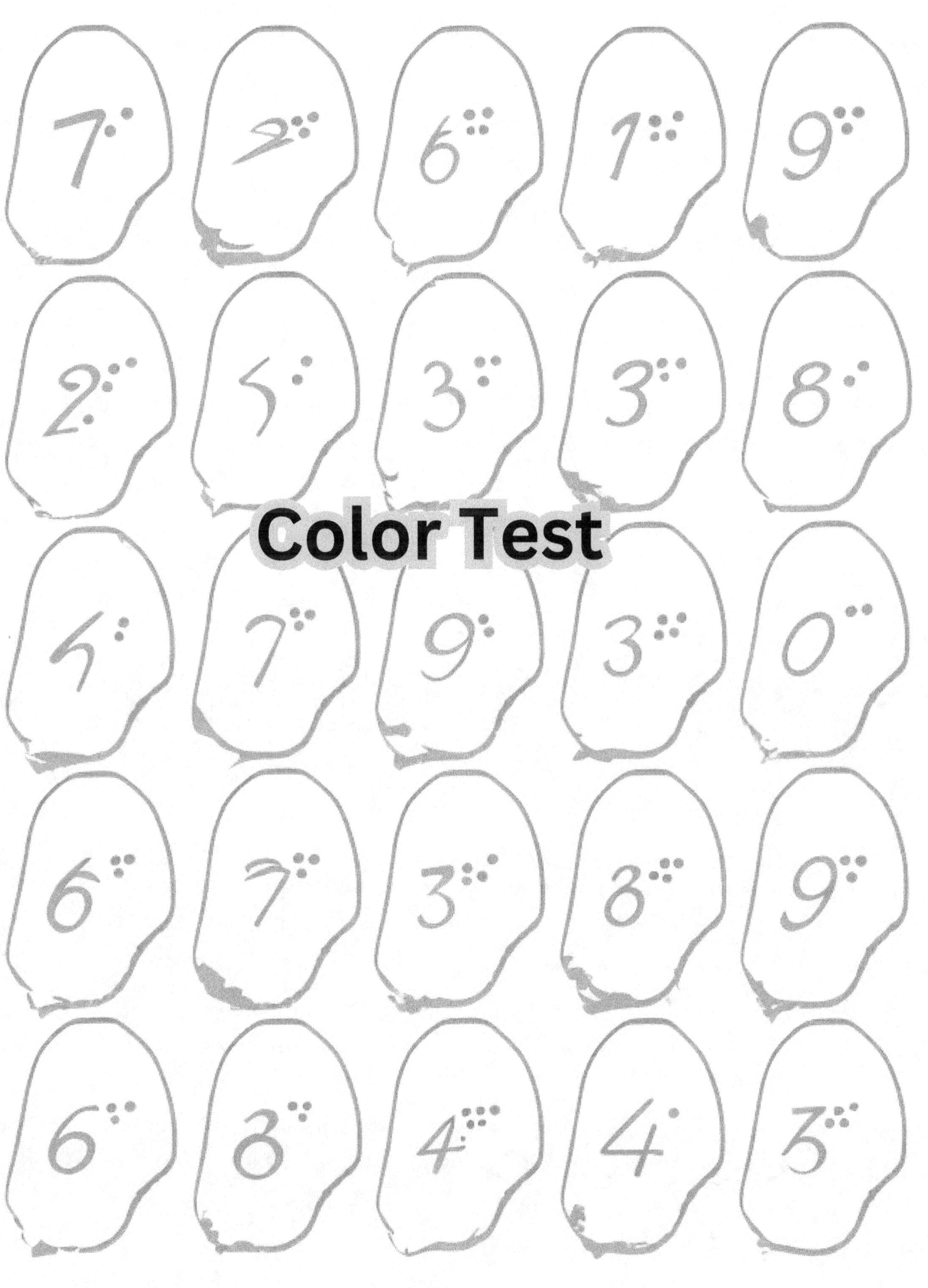
Color Test

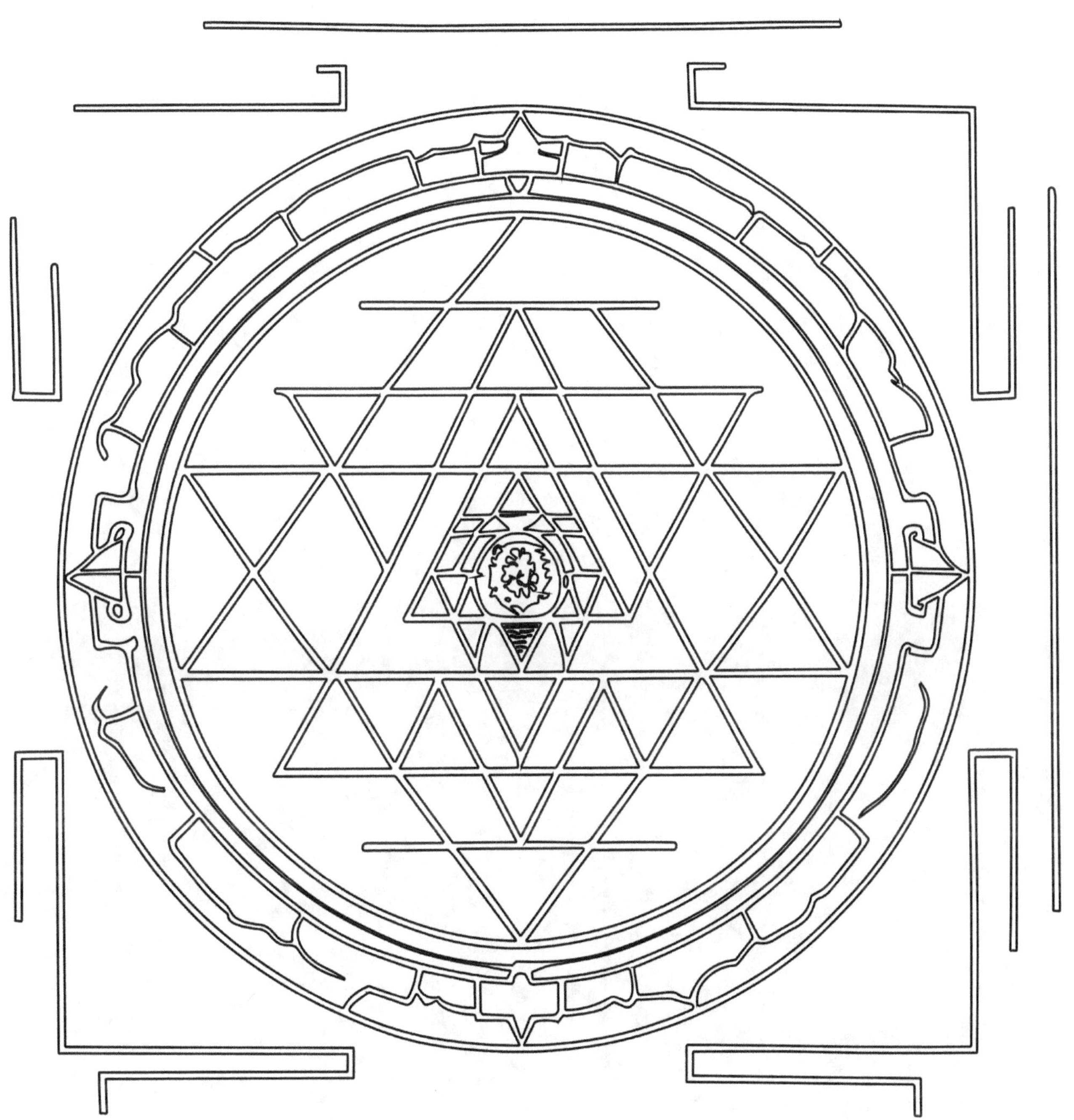

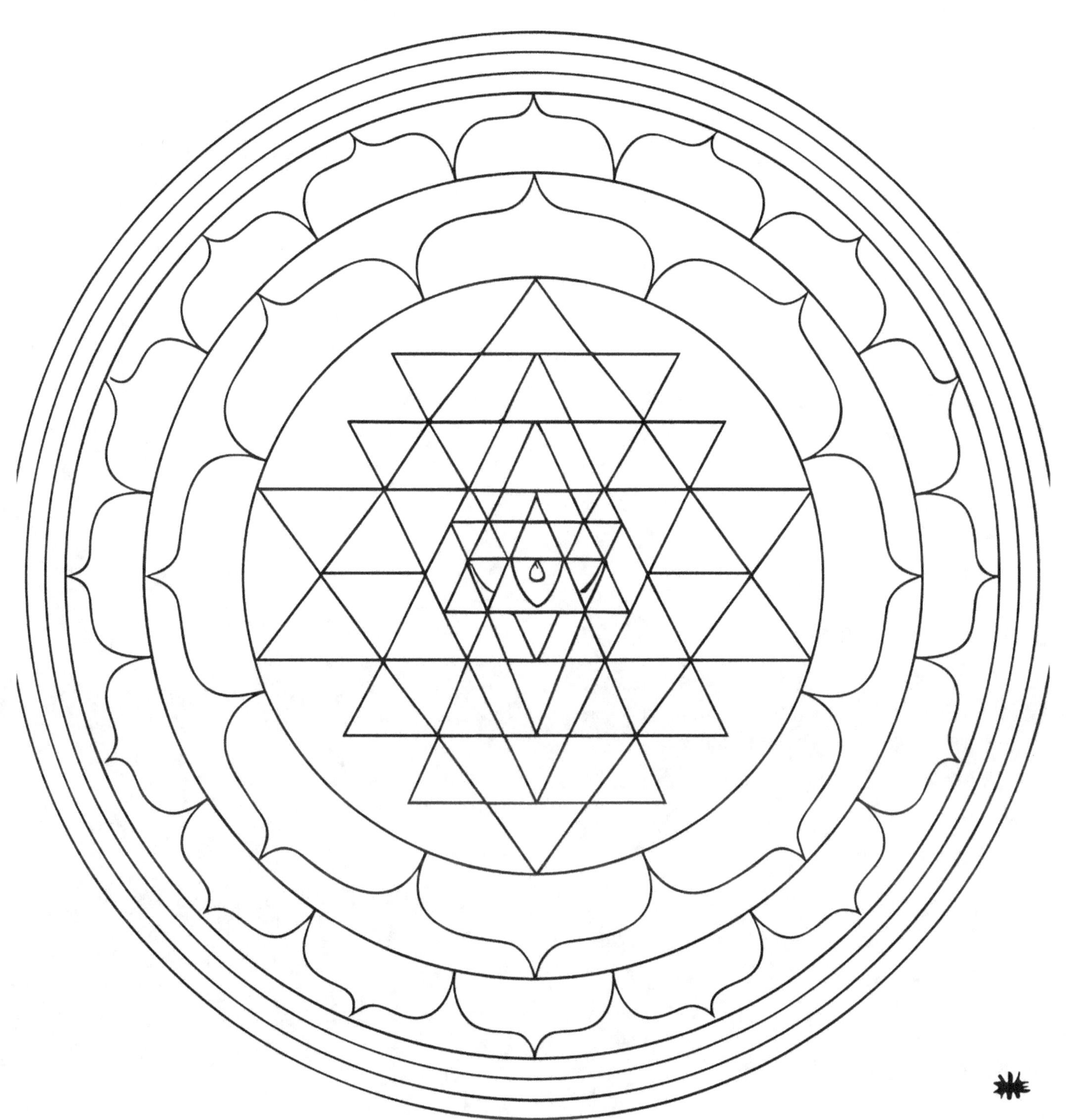

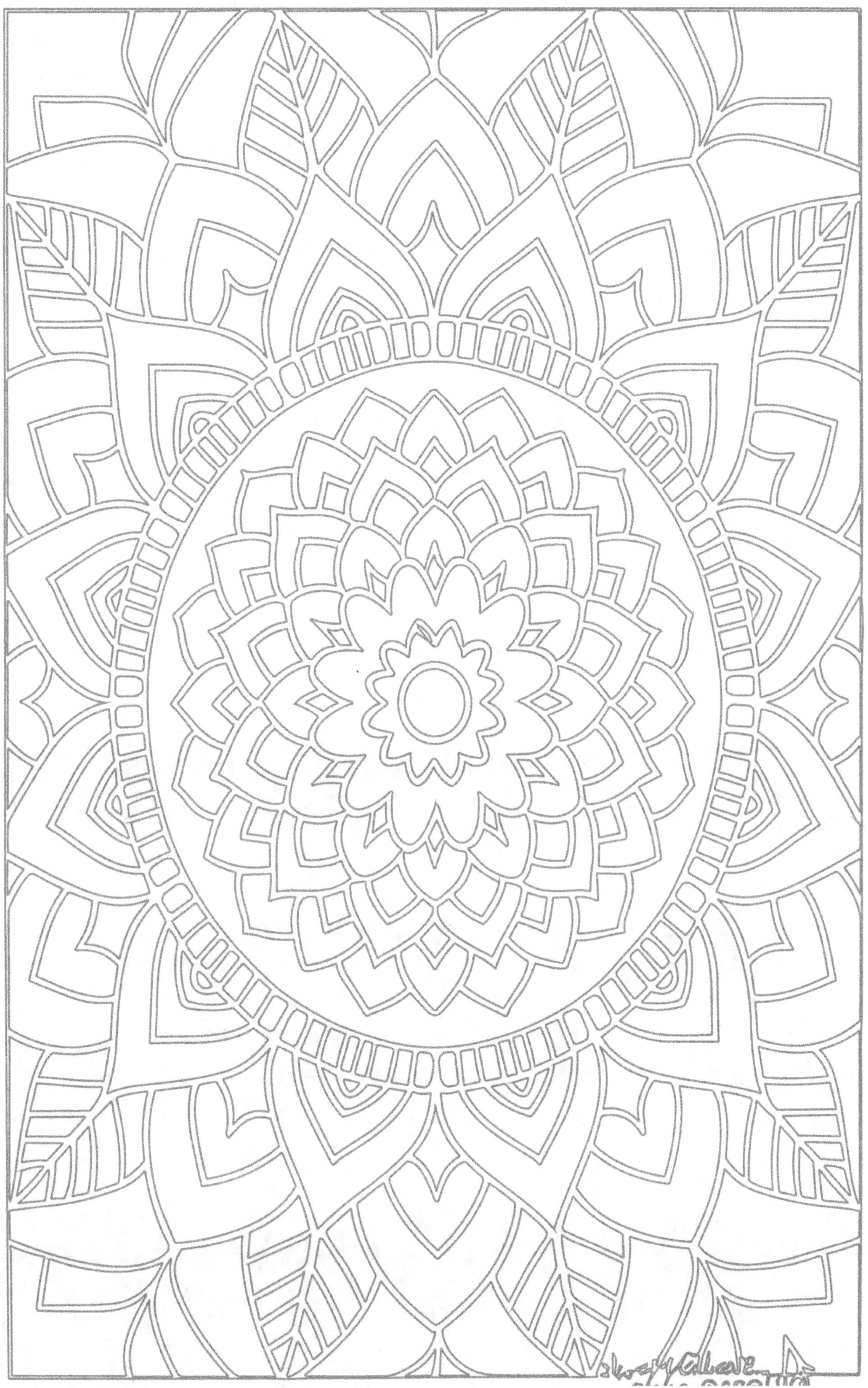

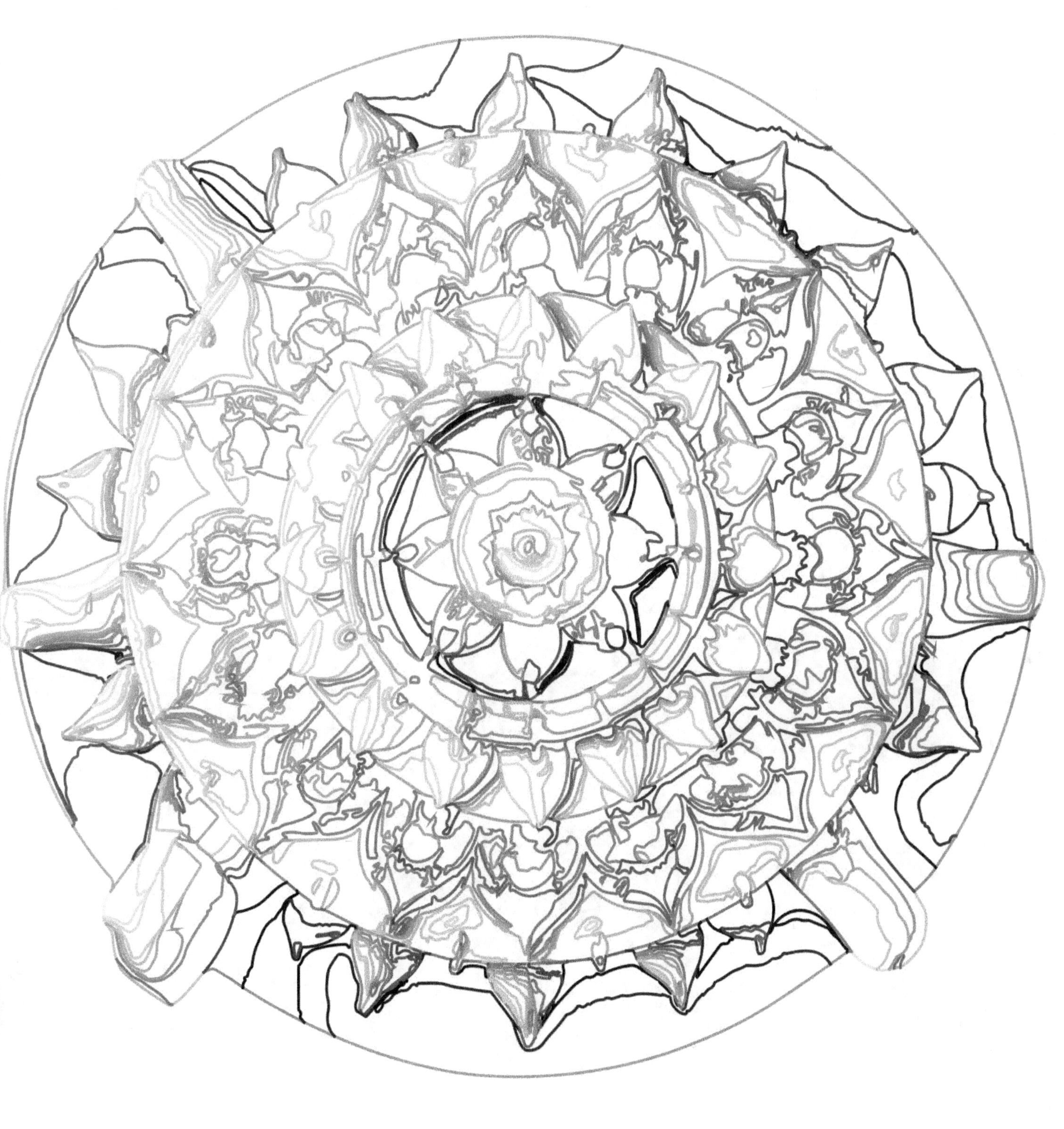

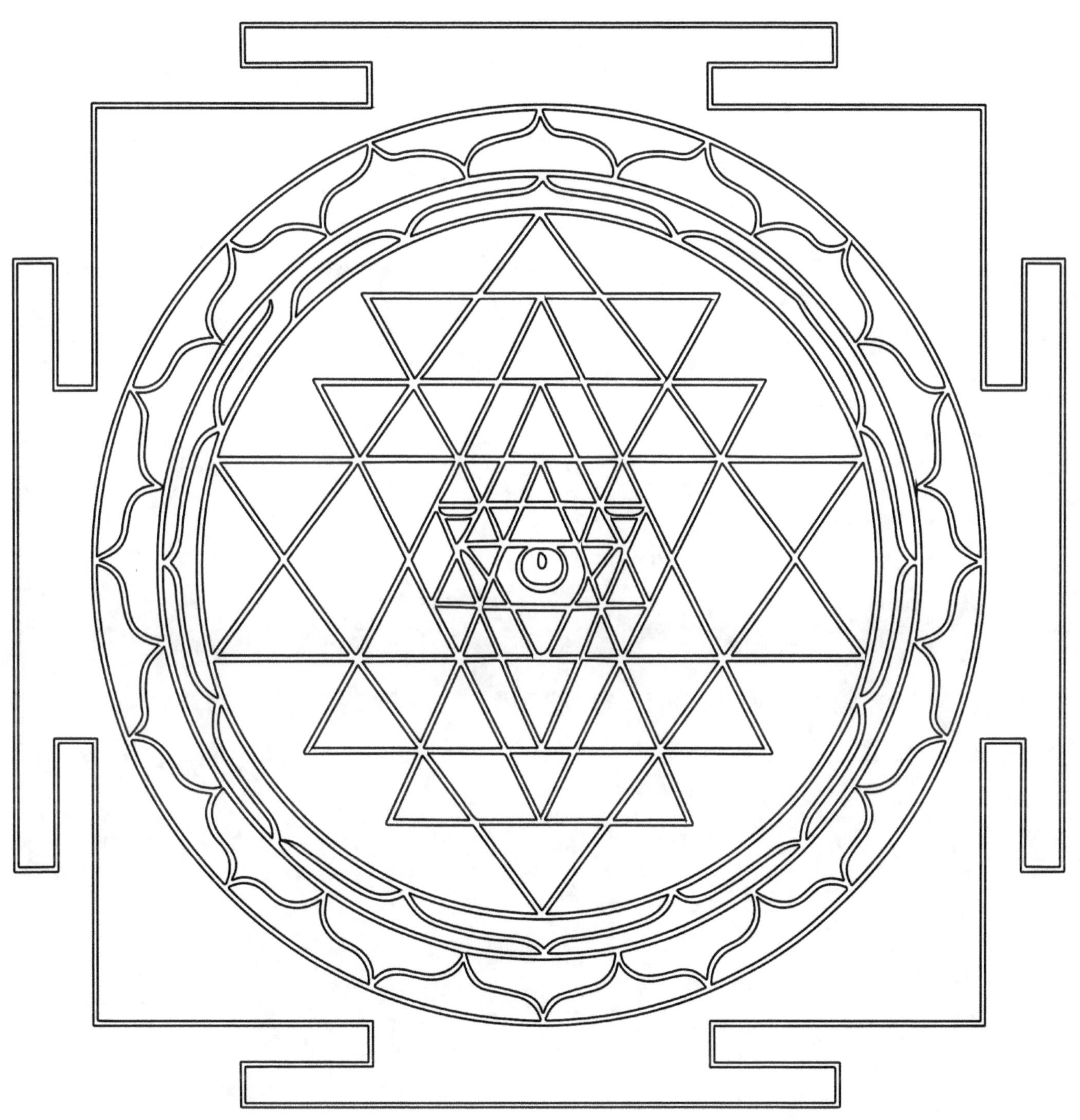

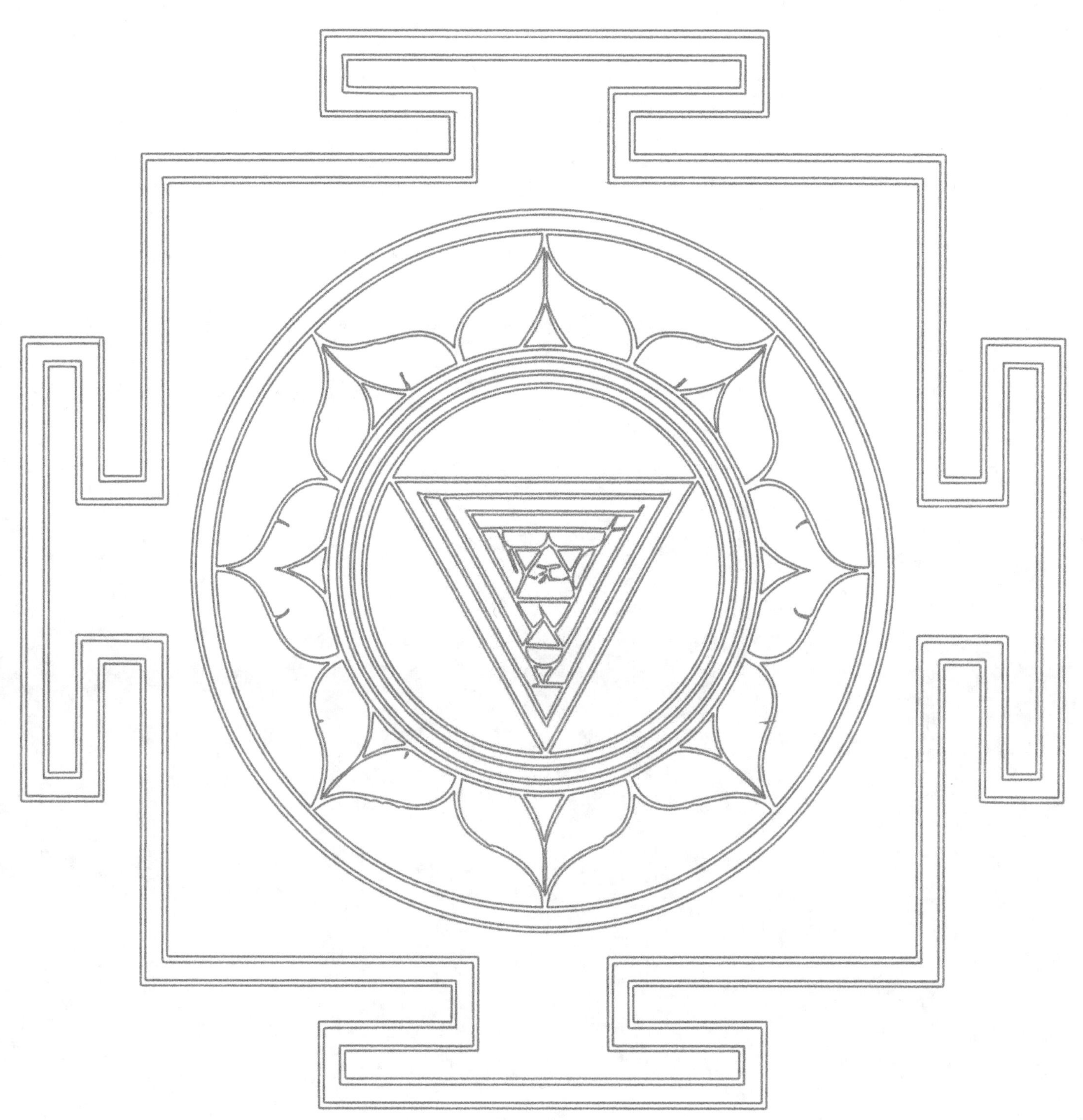

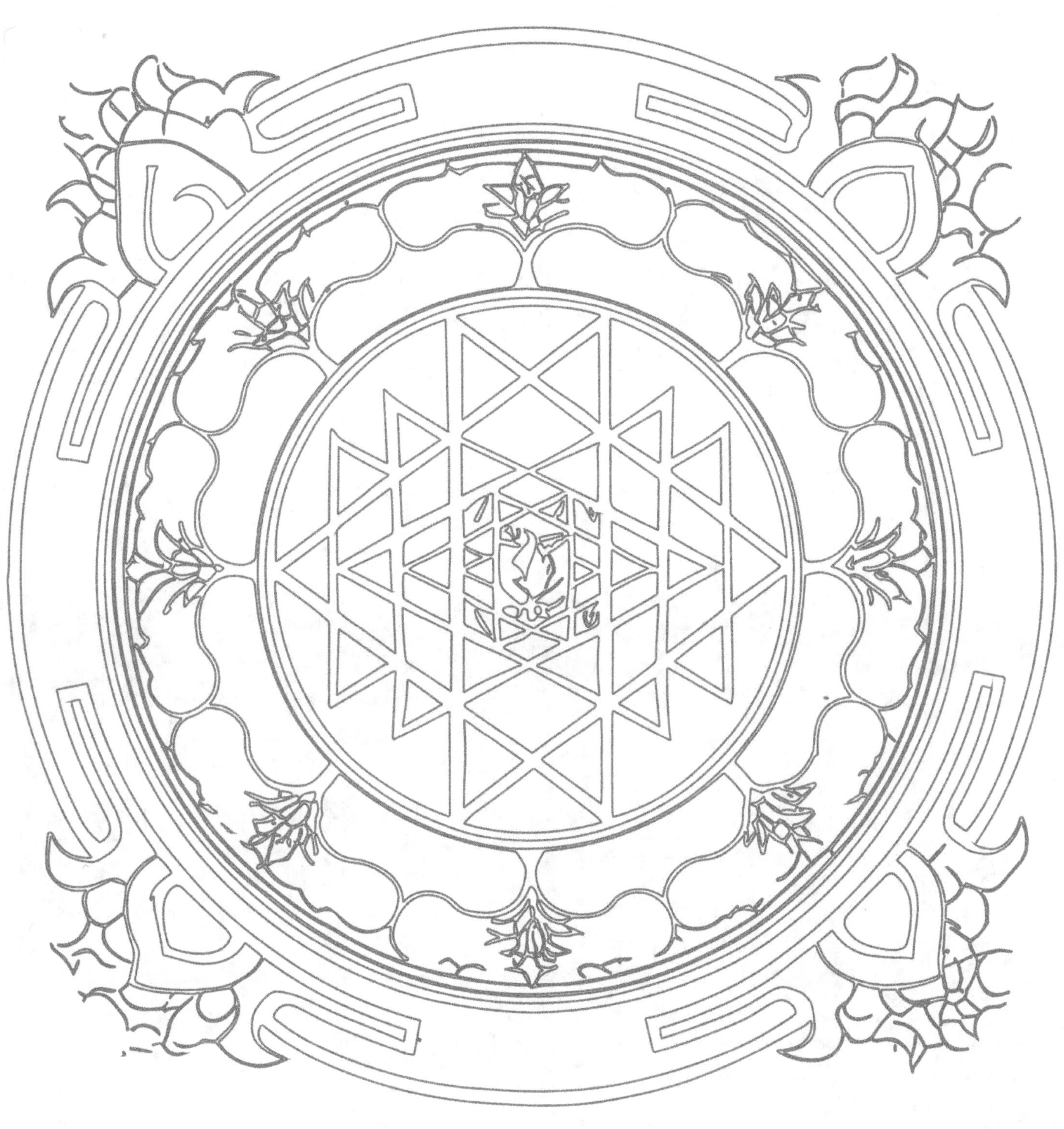

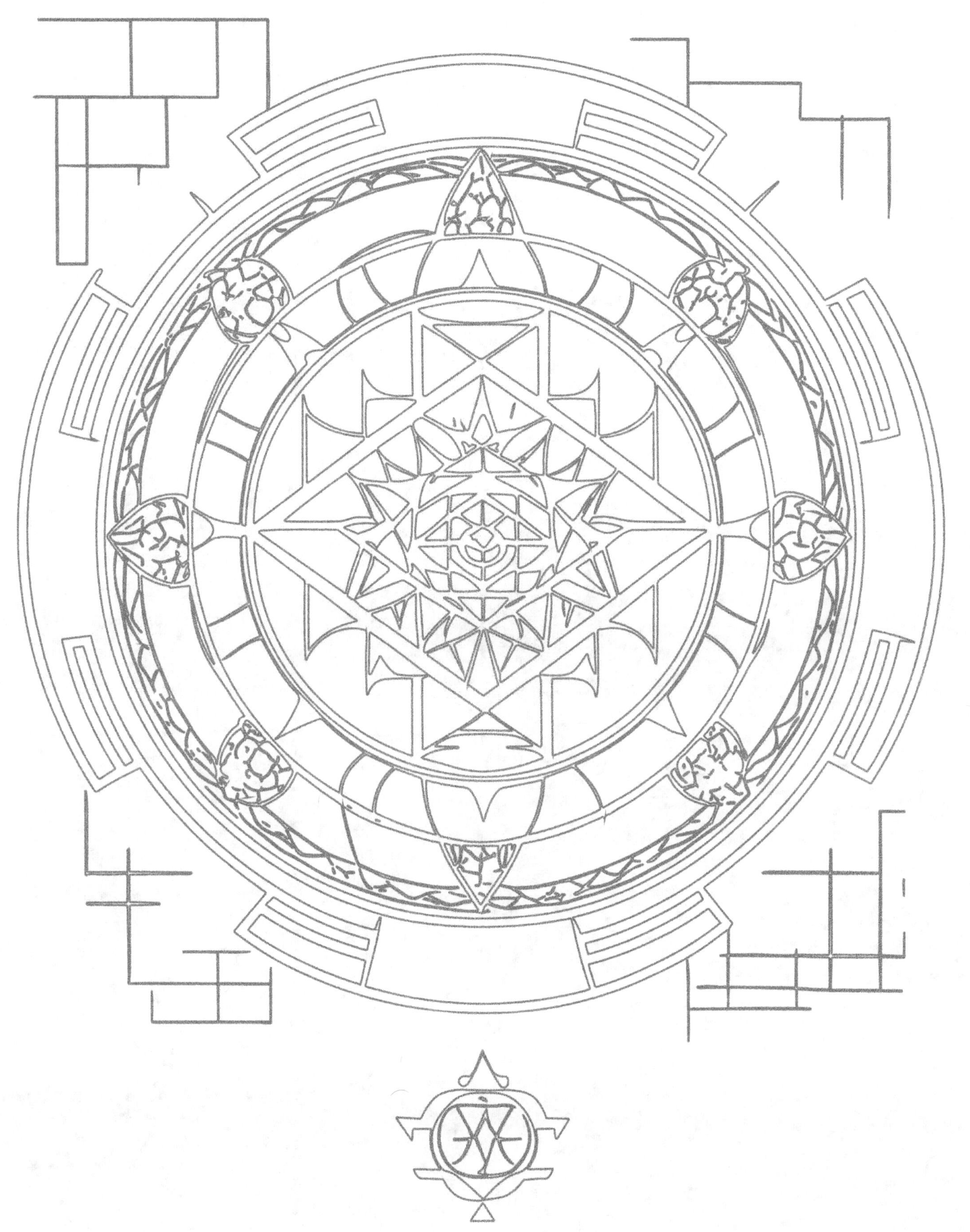

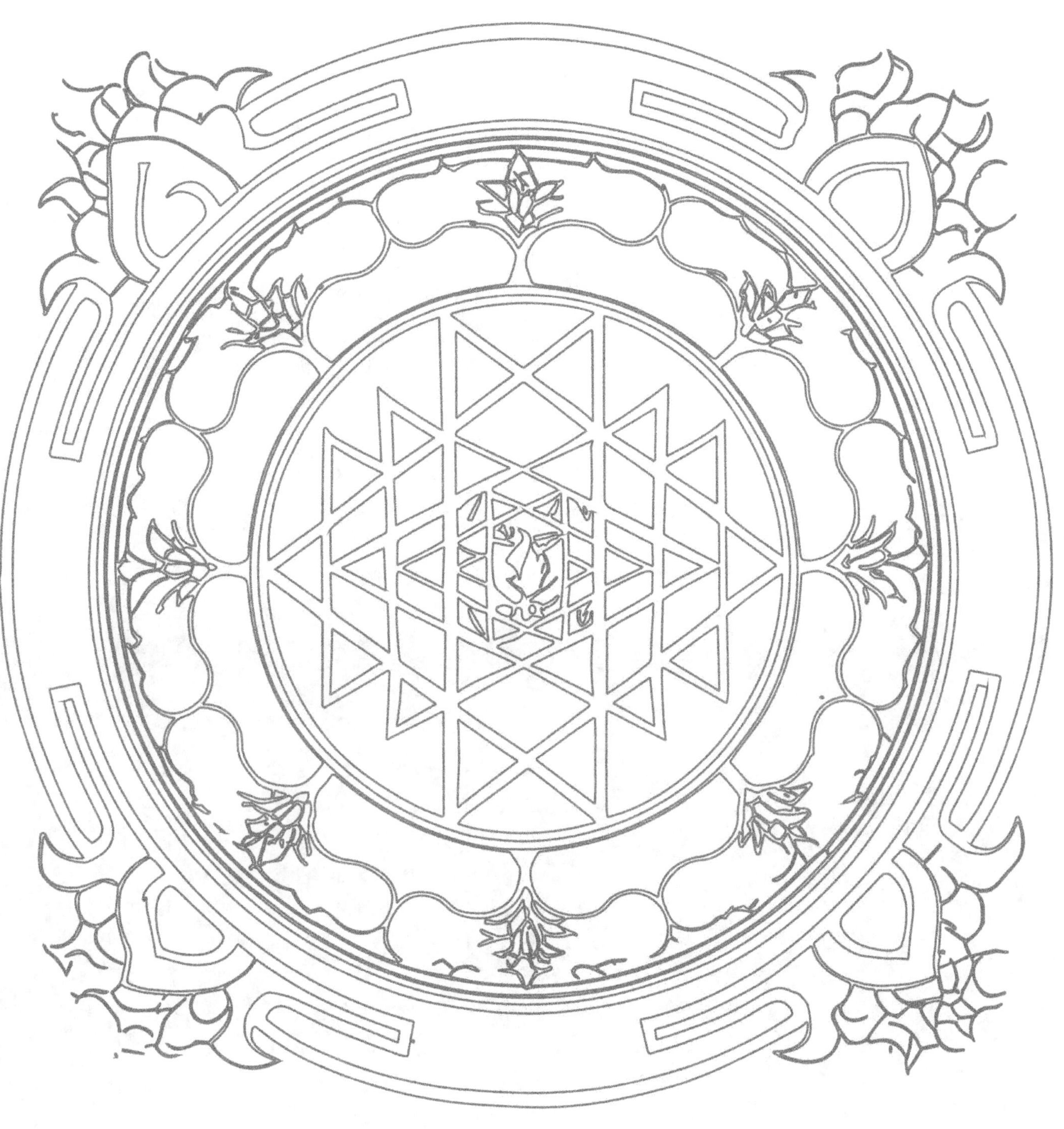

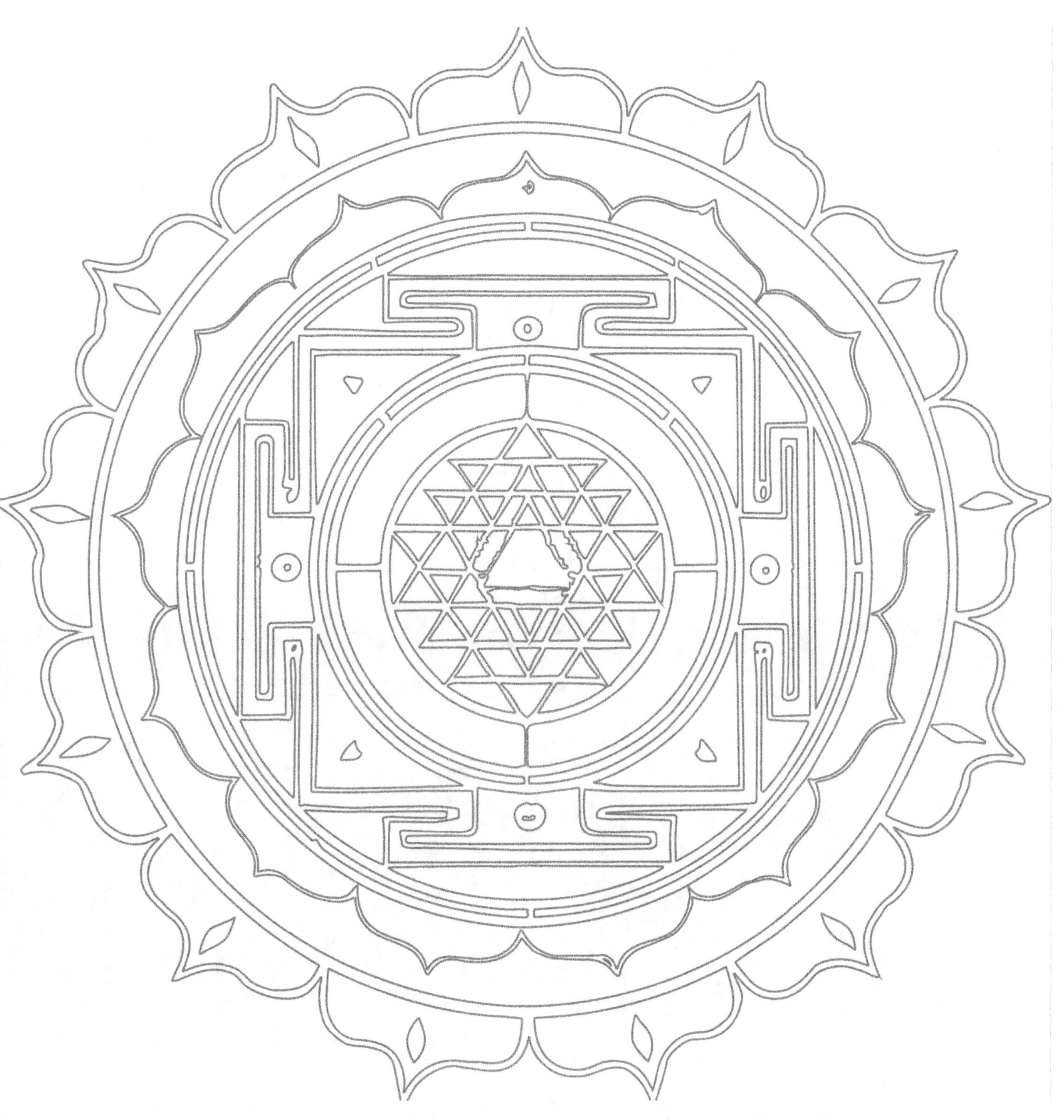

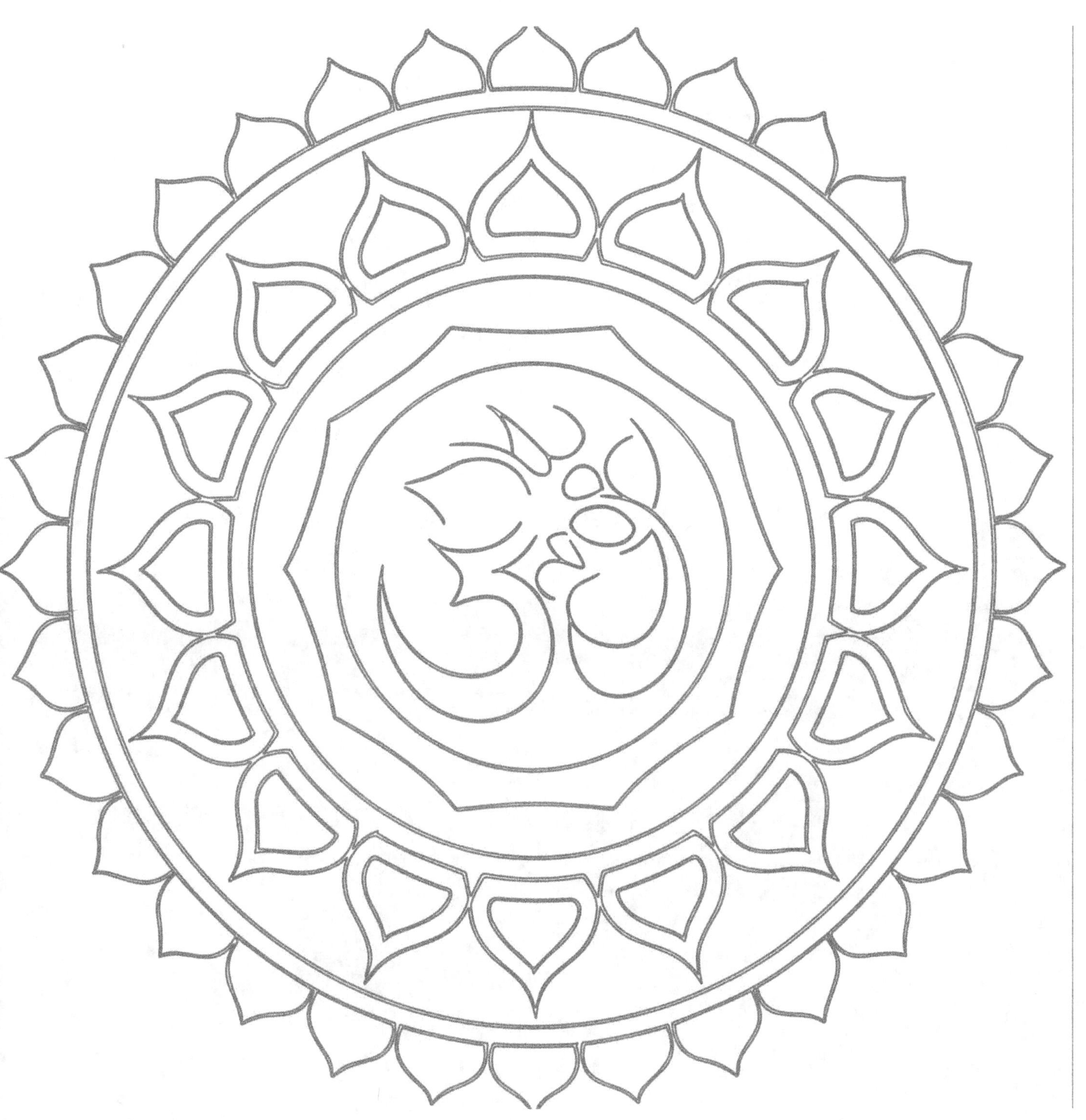

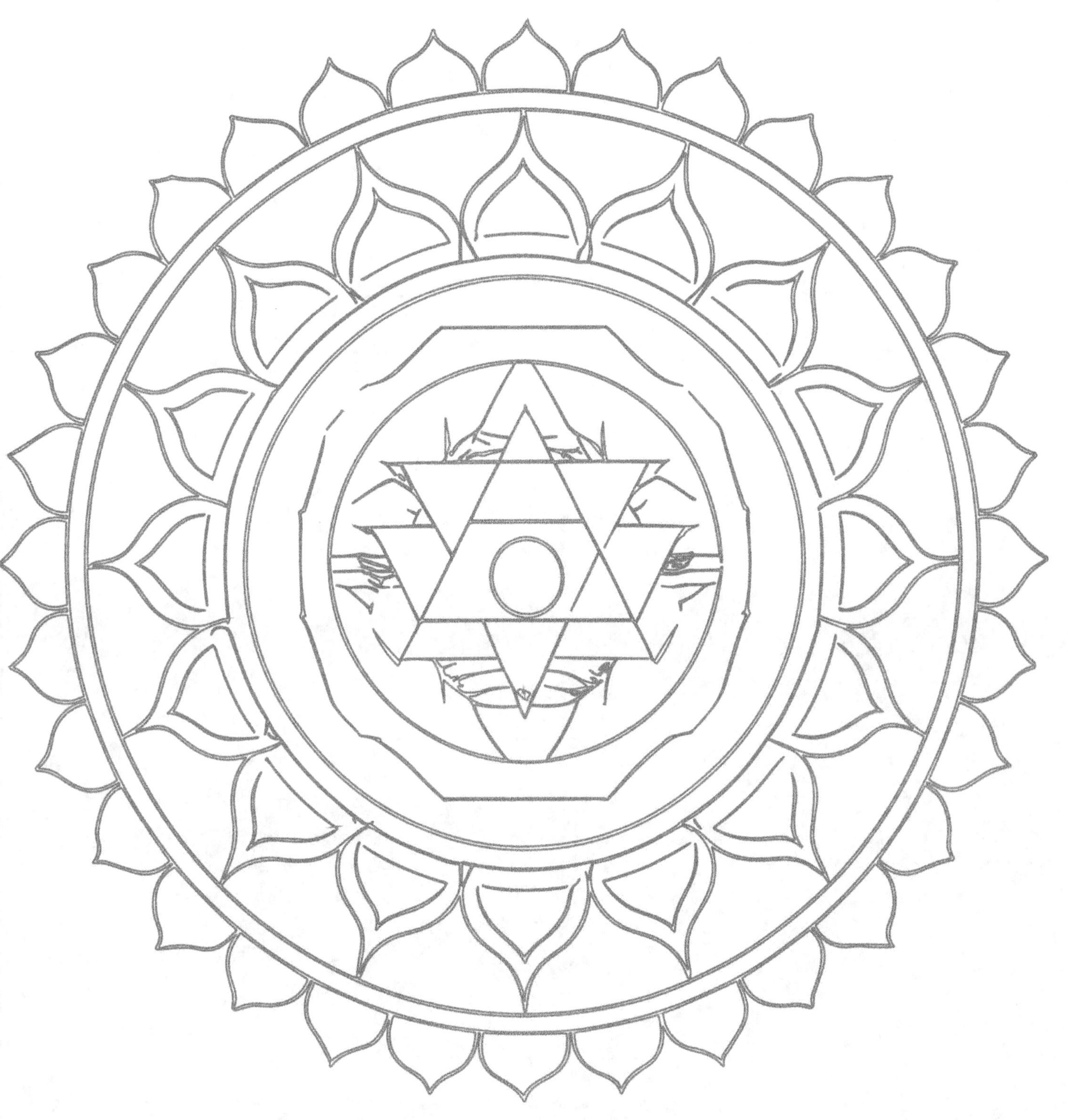

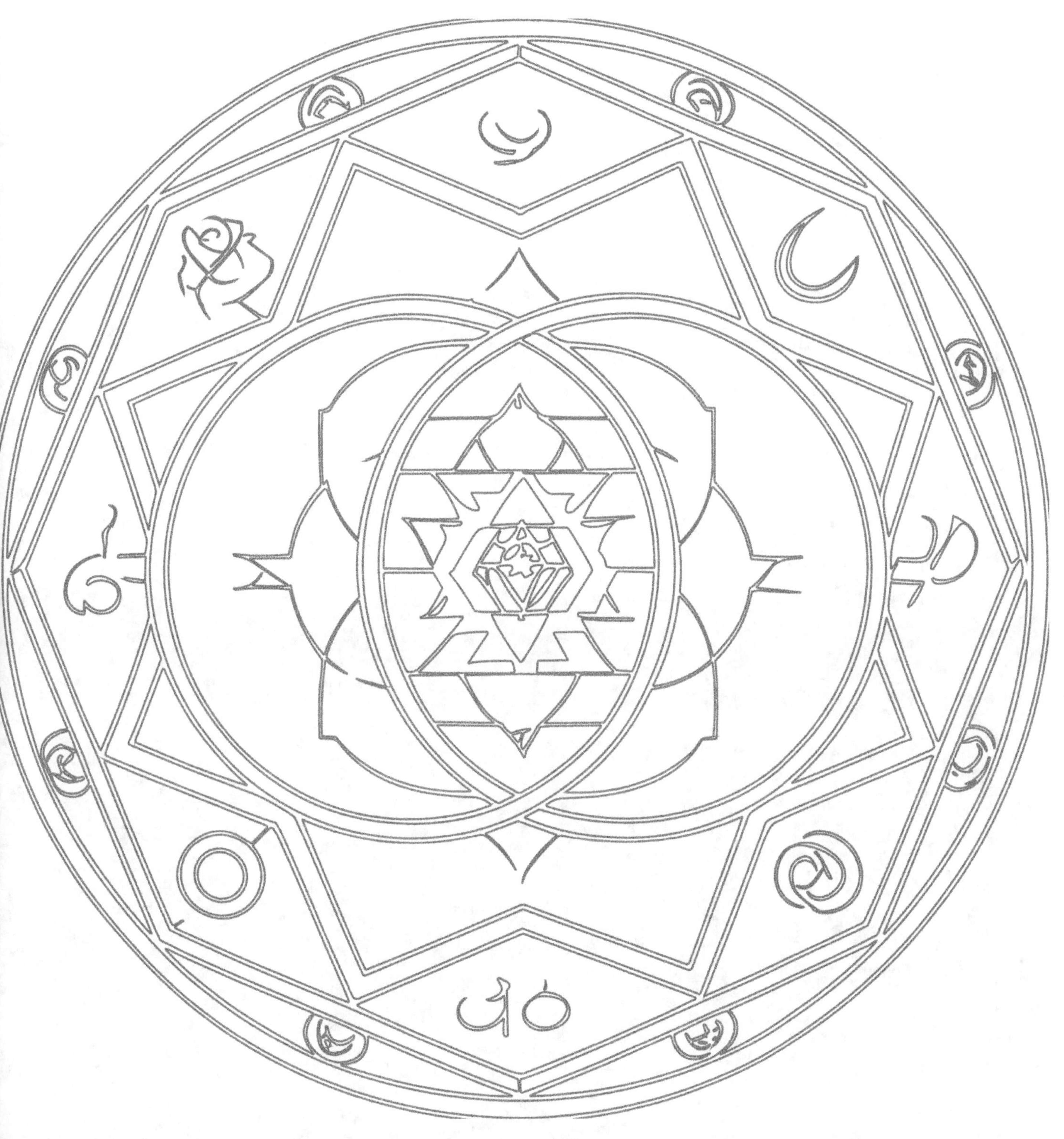

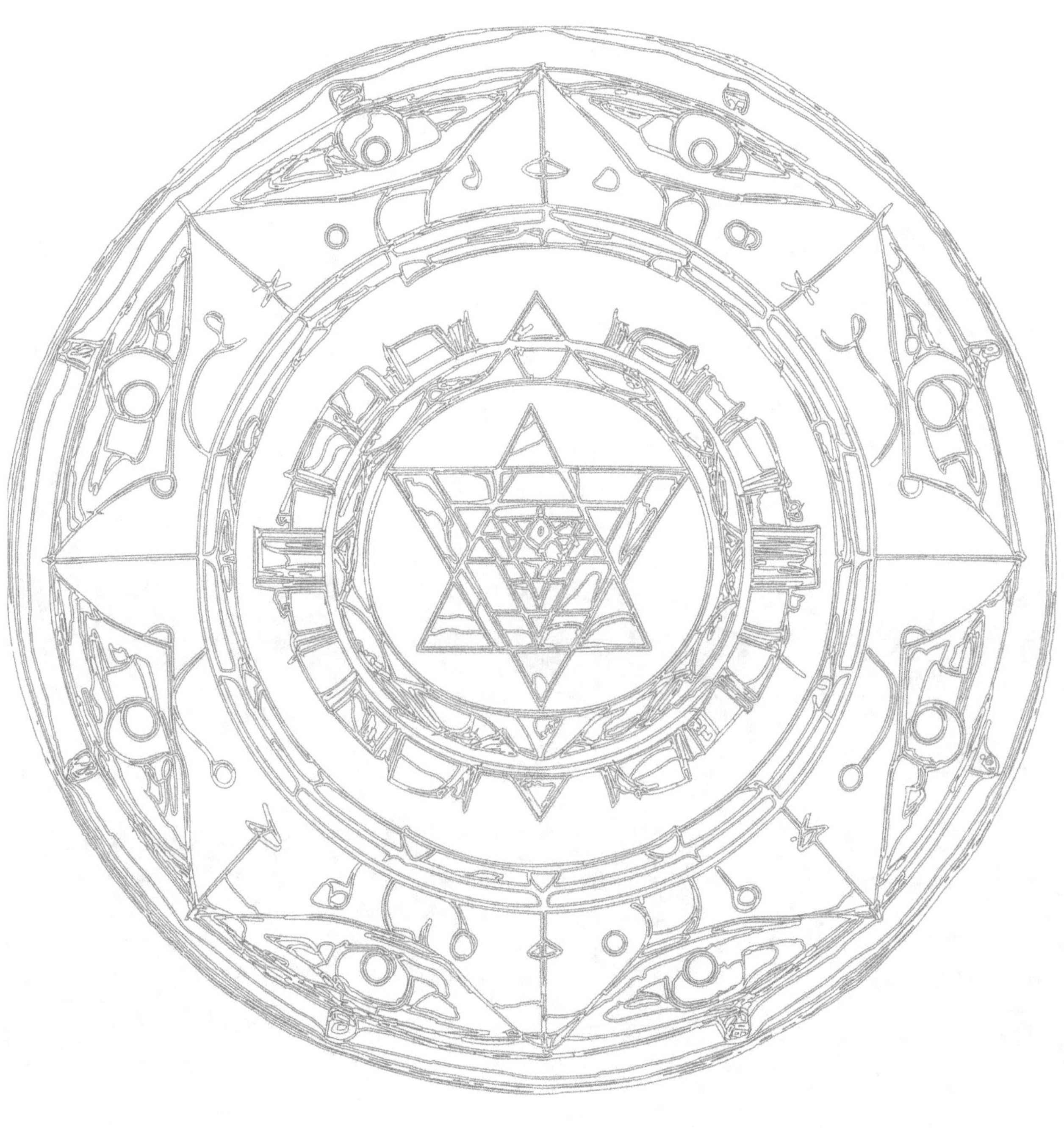

Note : Use your imagination to draw the boundary and fill it with colors.

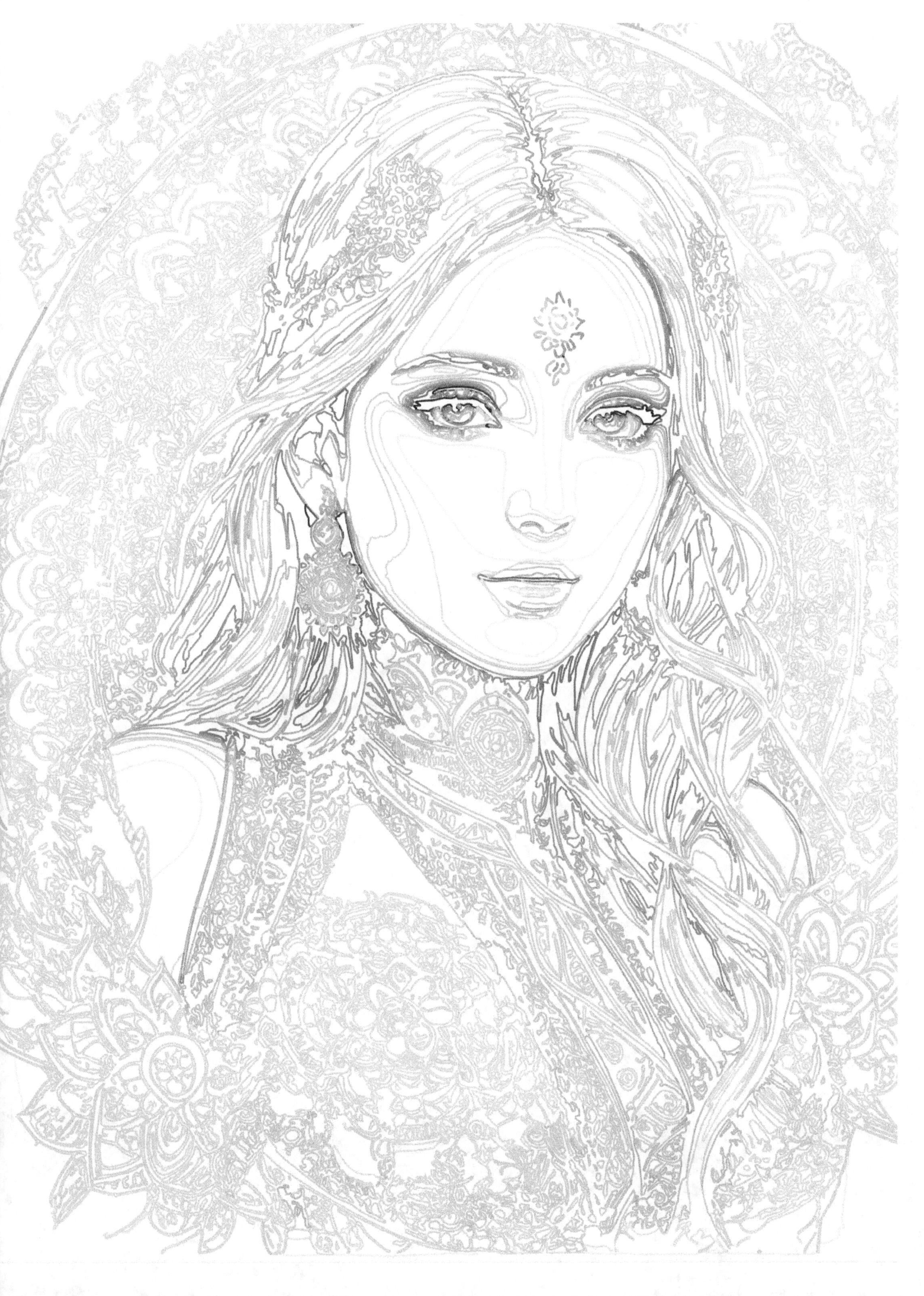

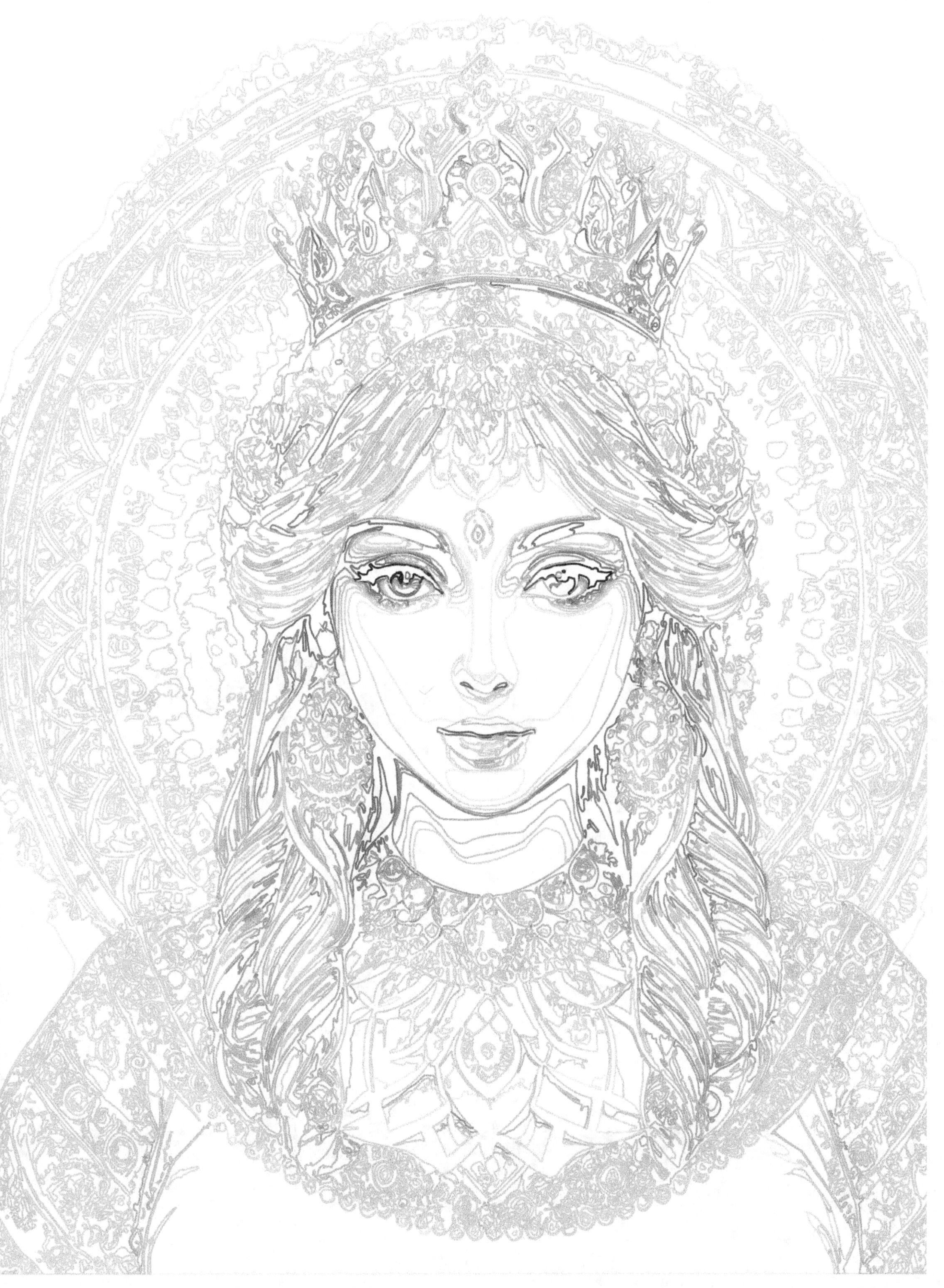

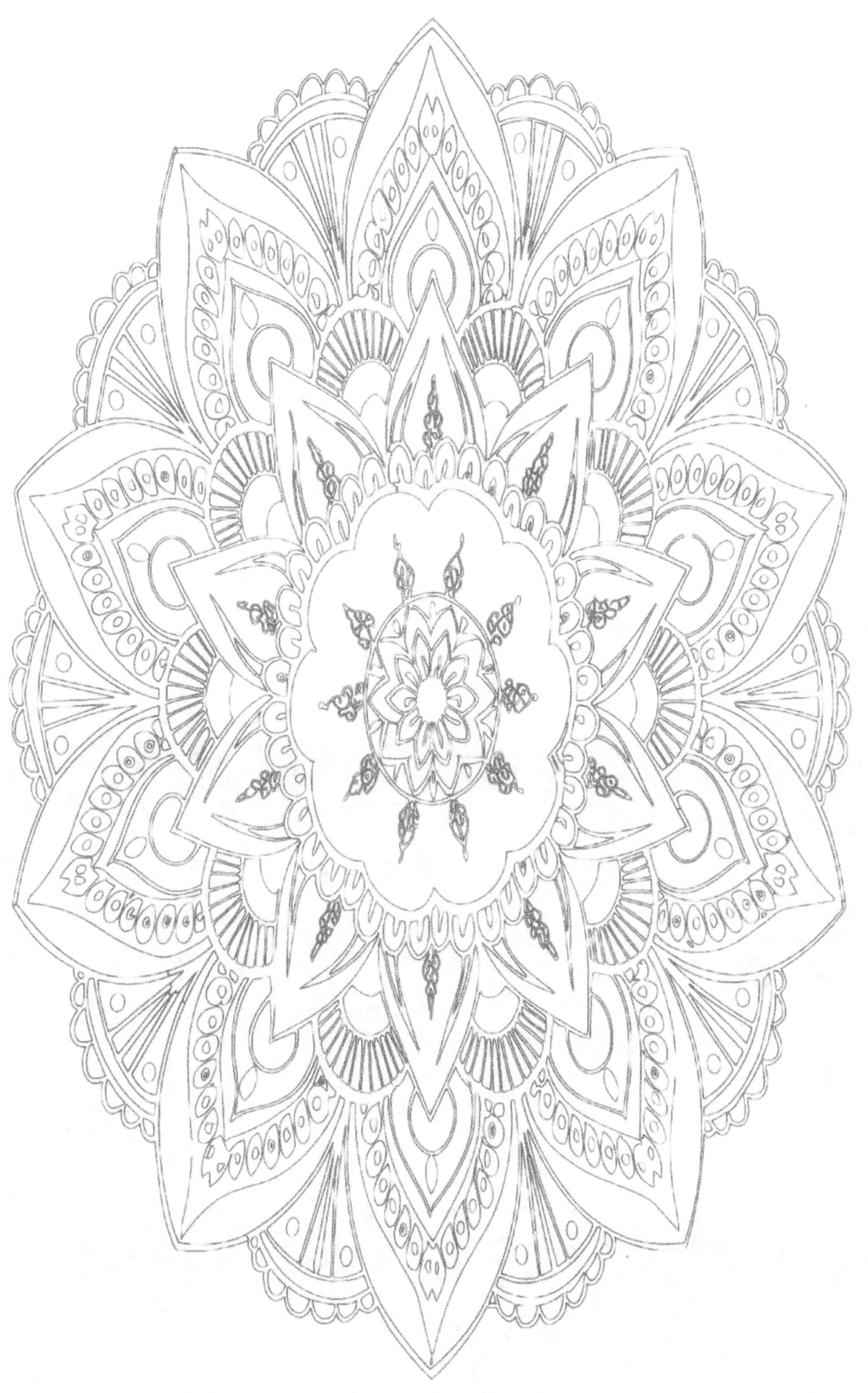

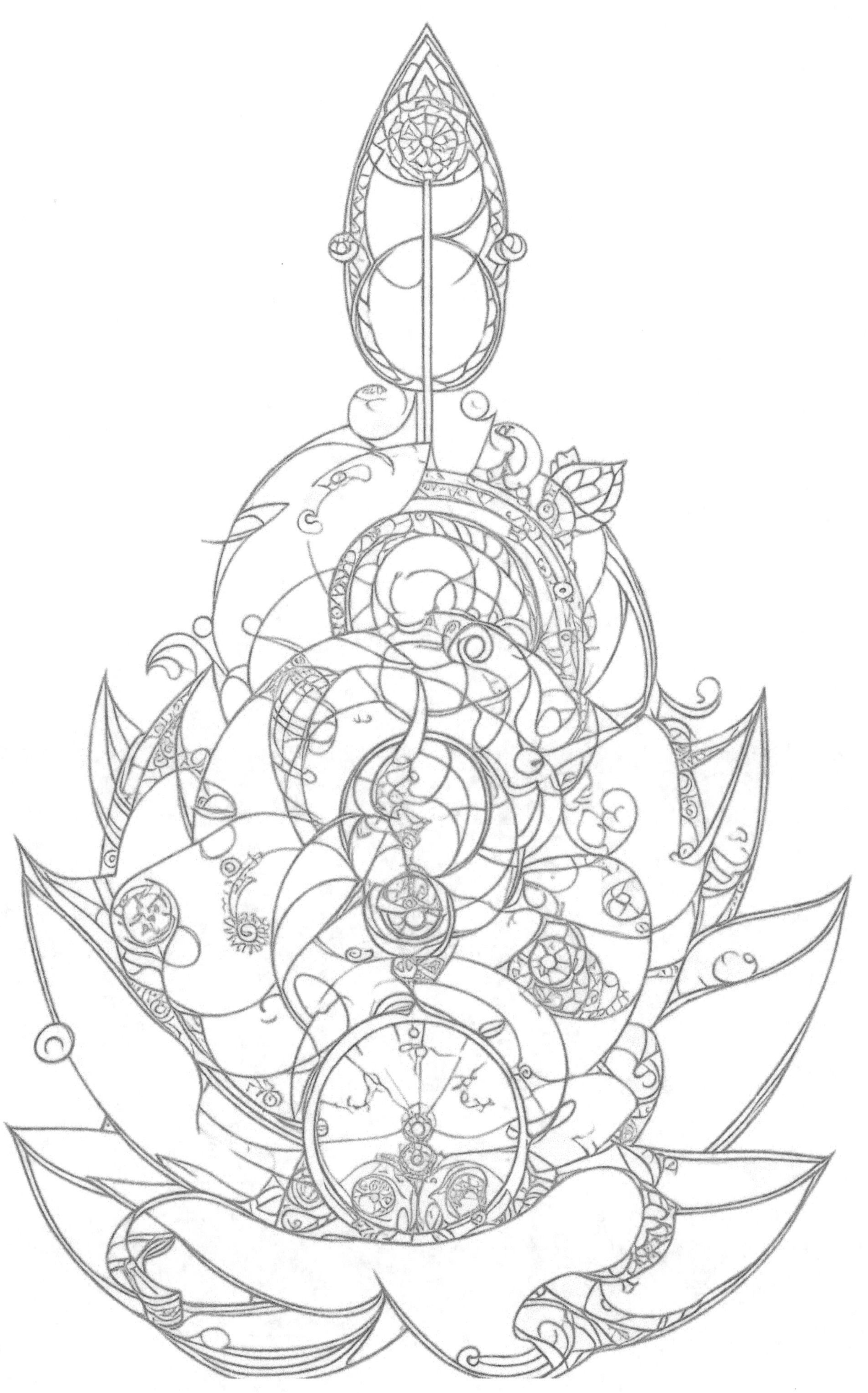

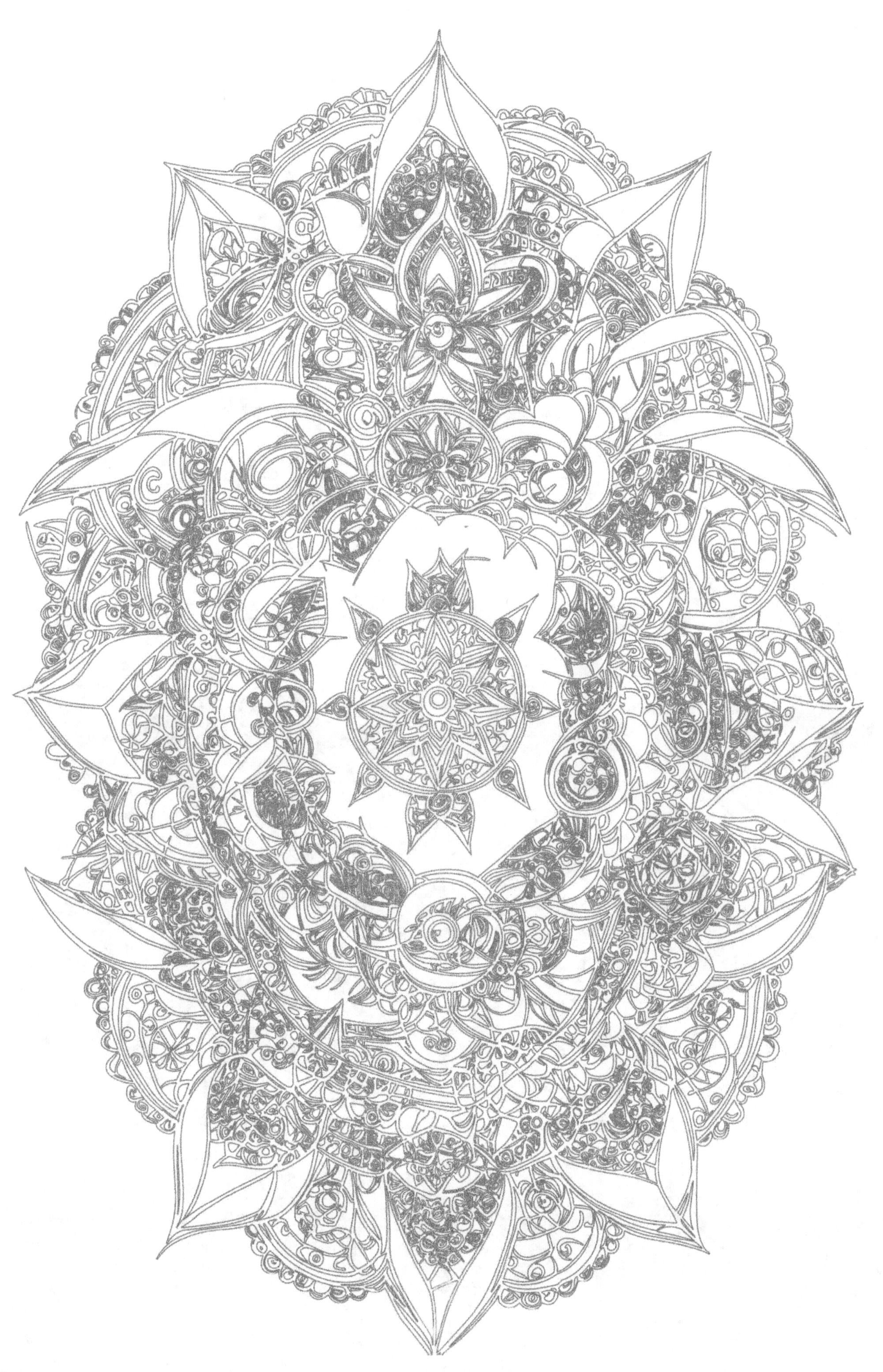

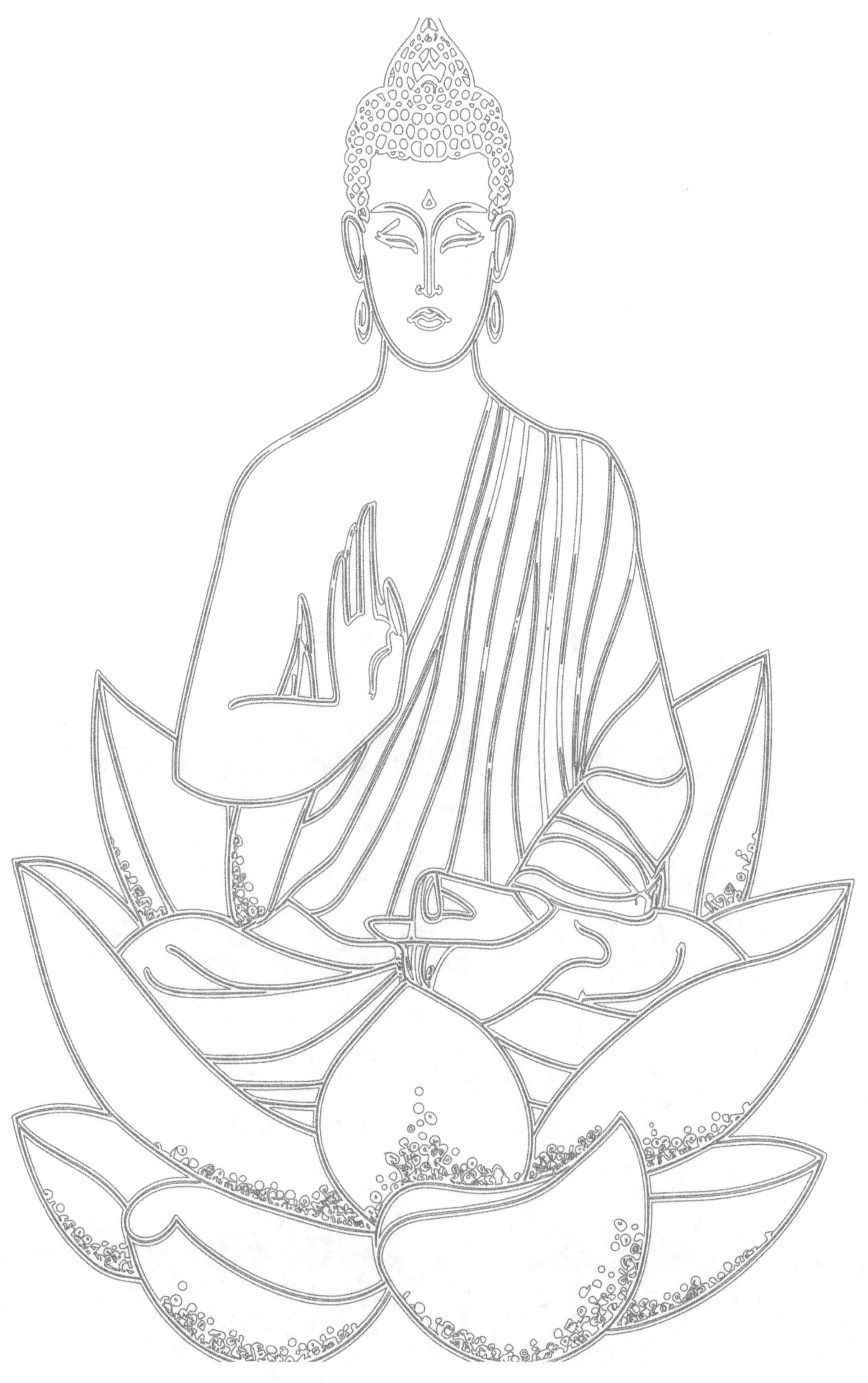

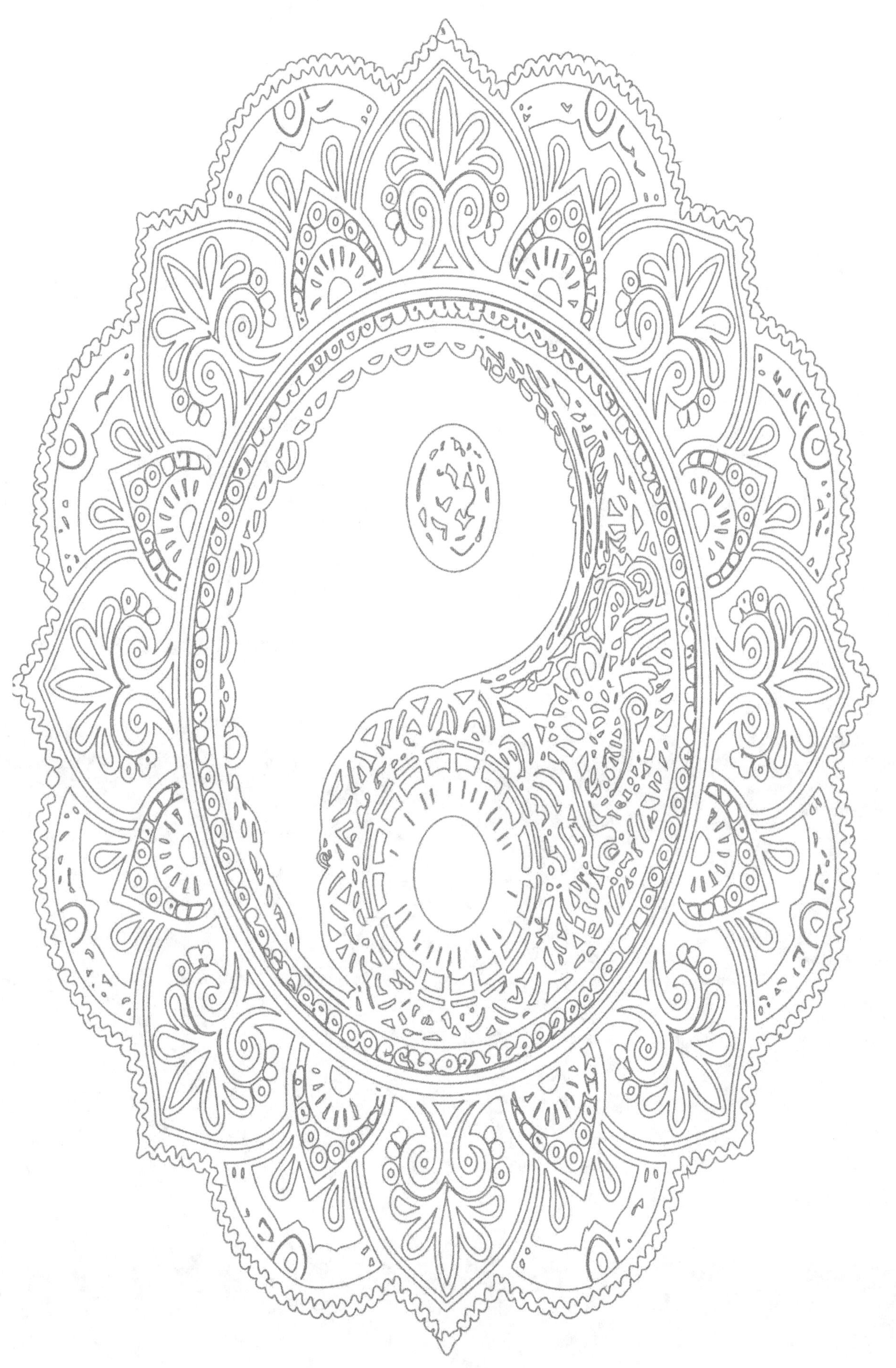

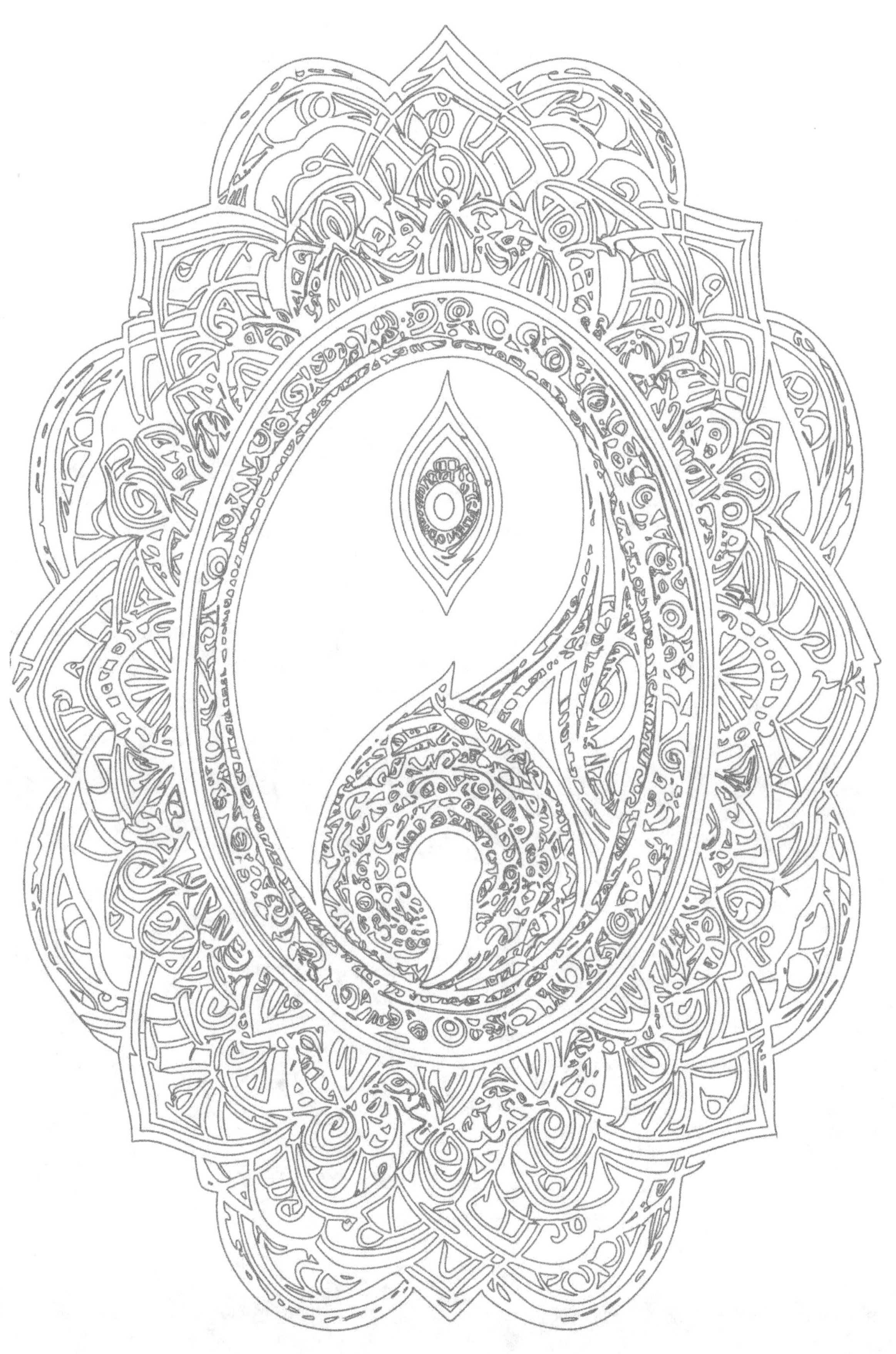

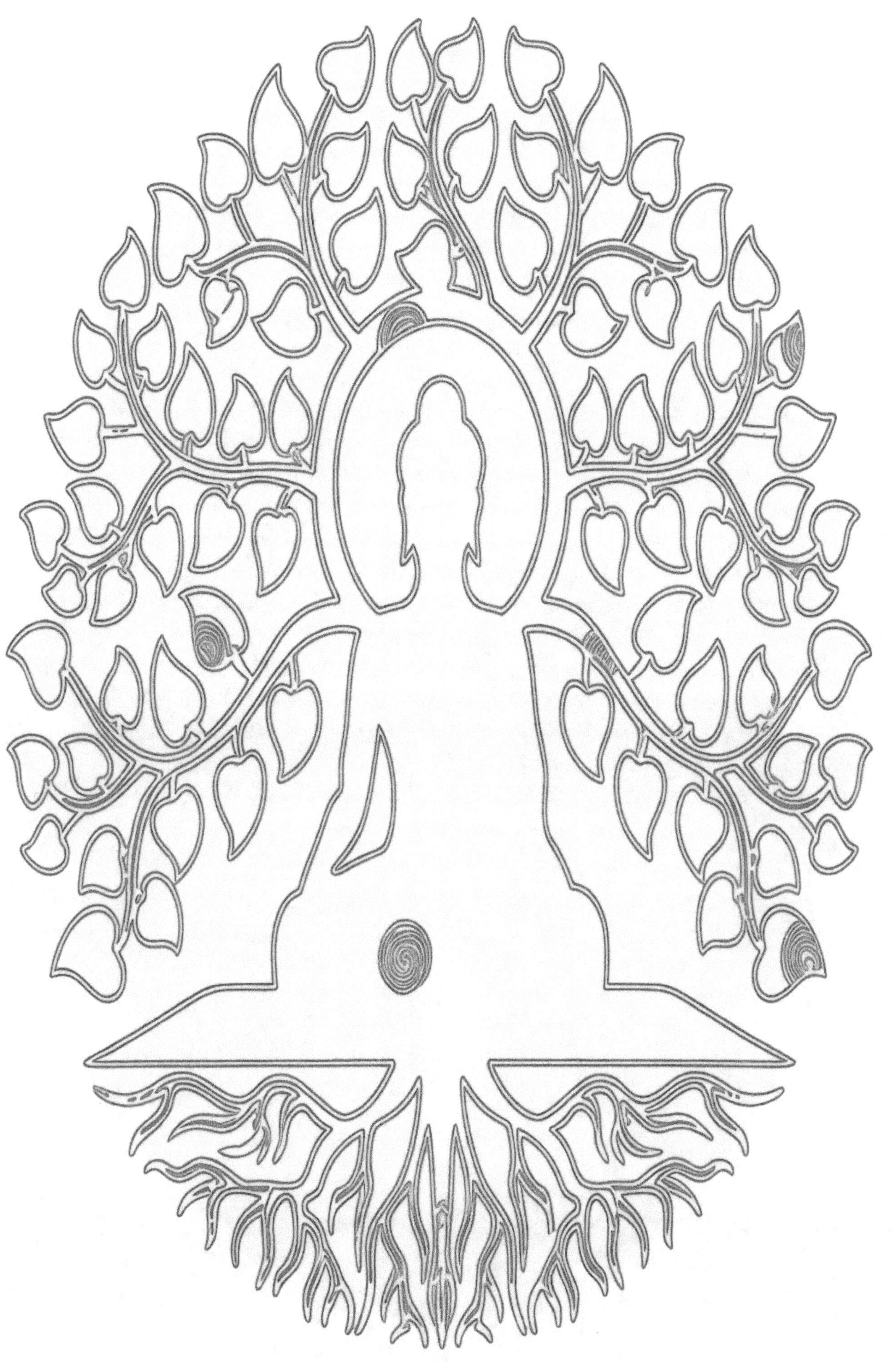

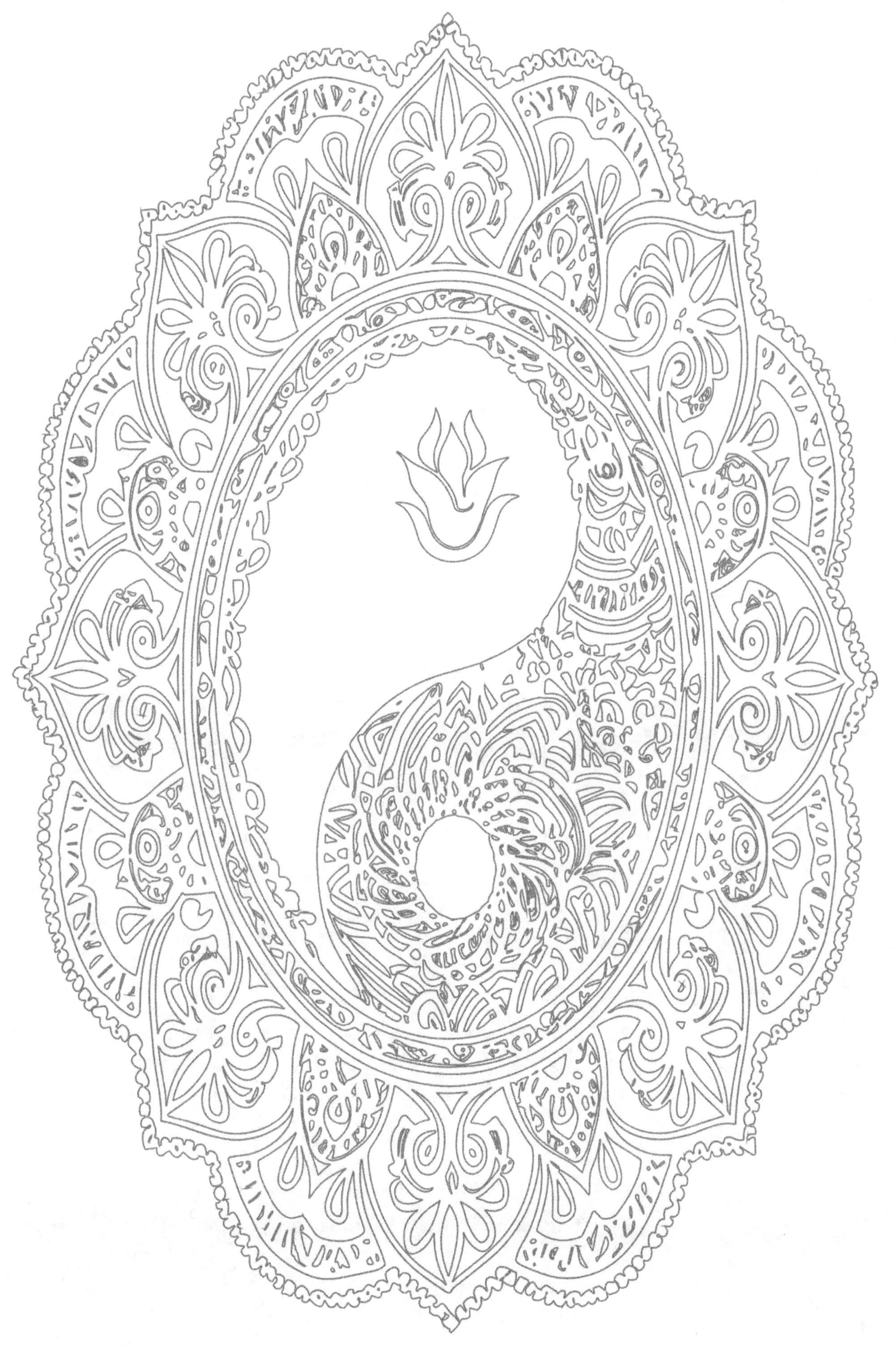

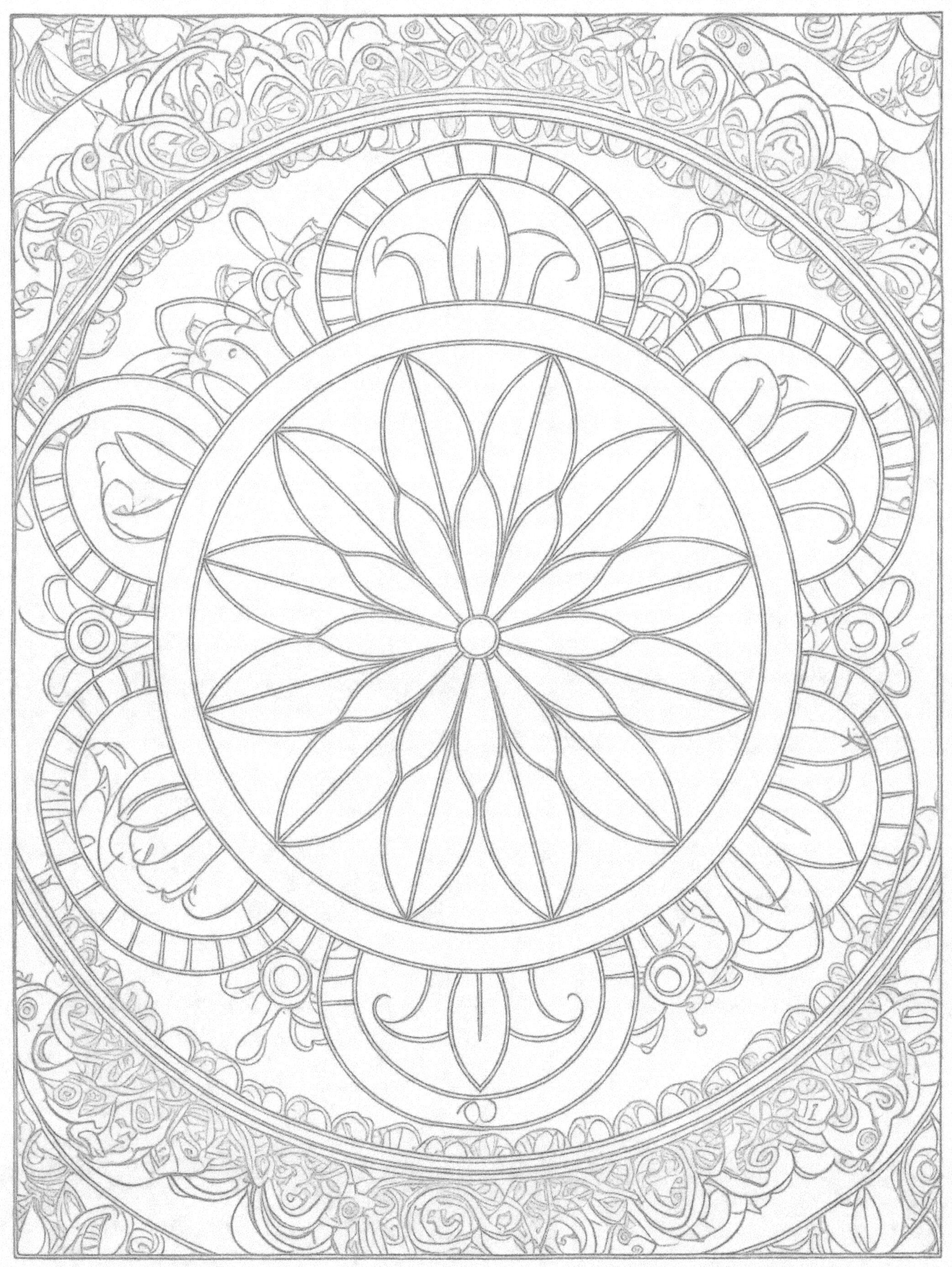

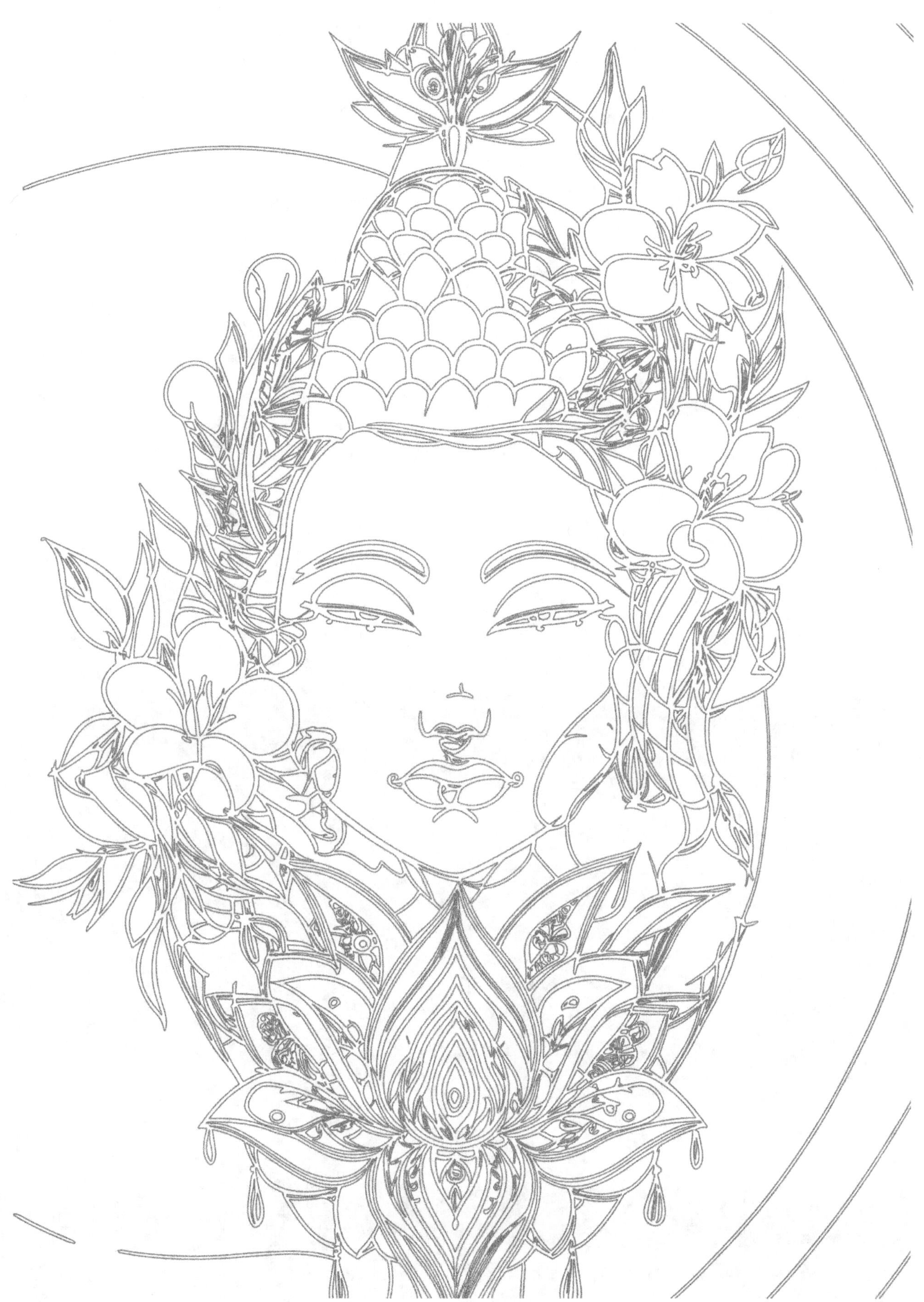

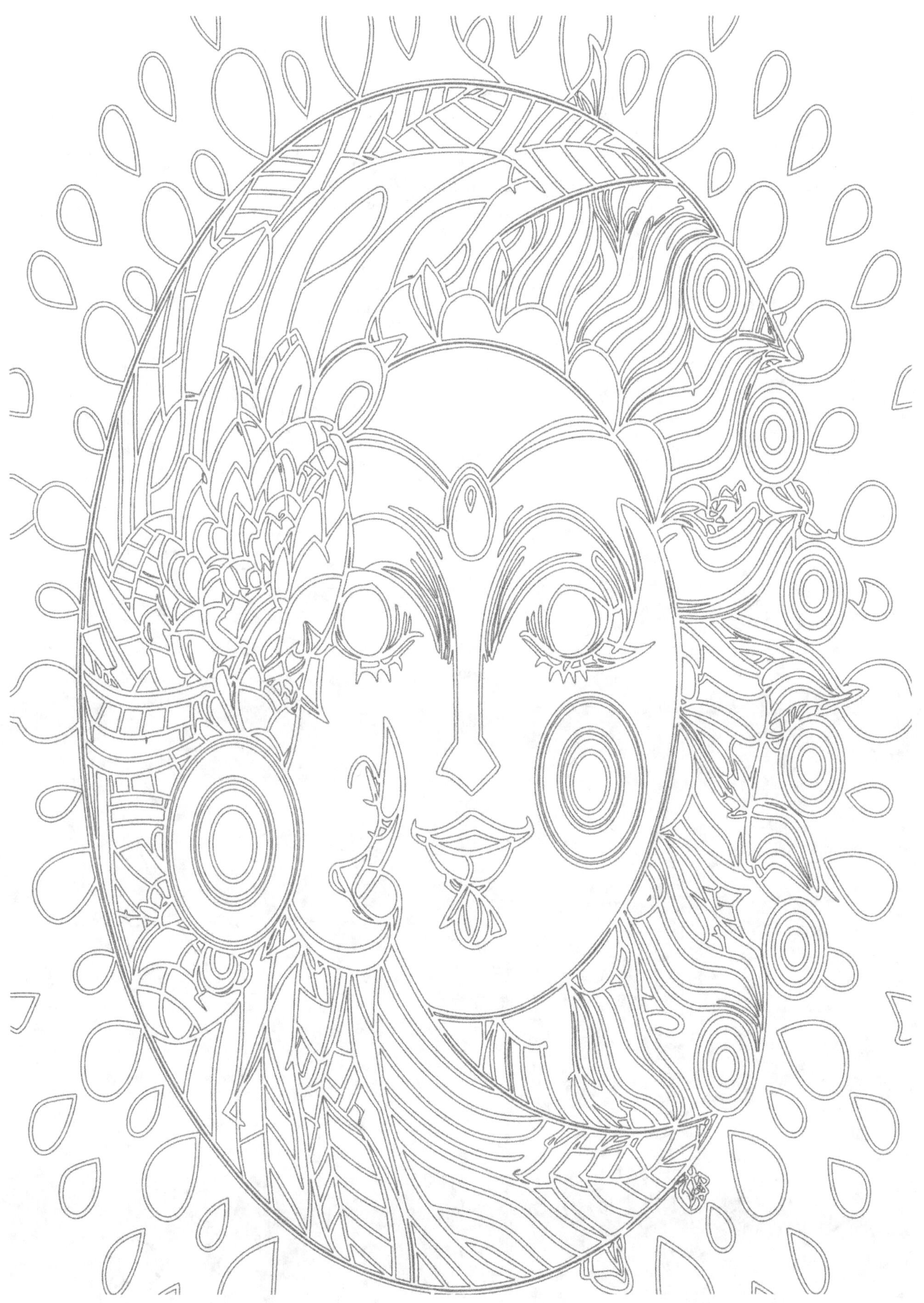

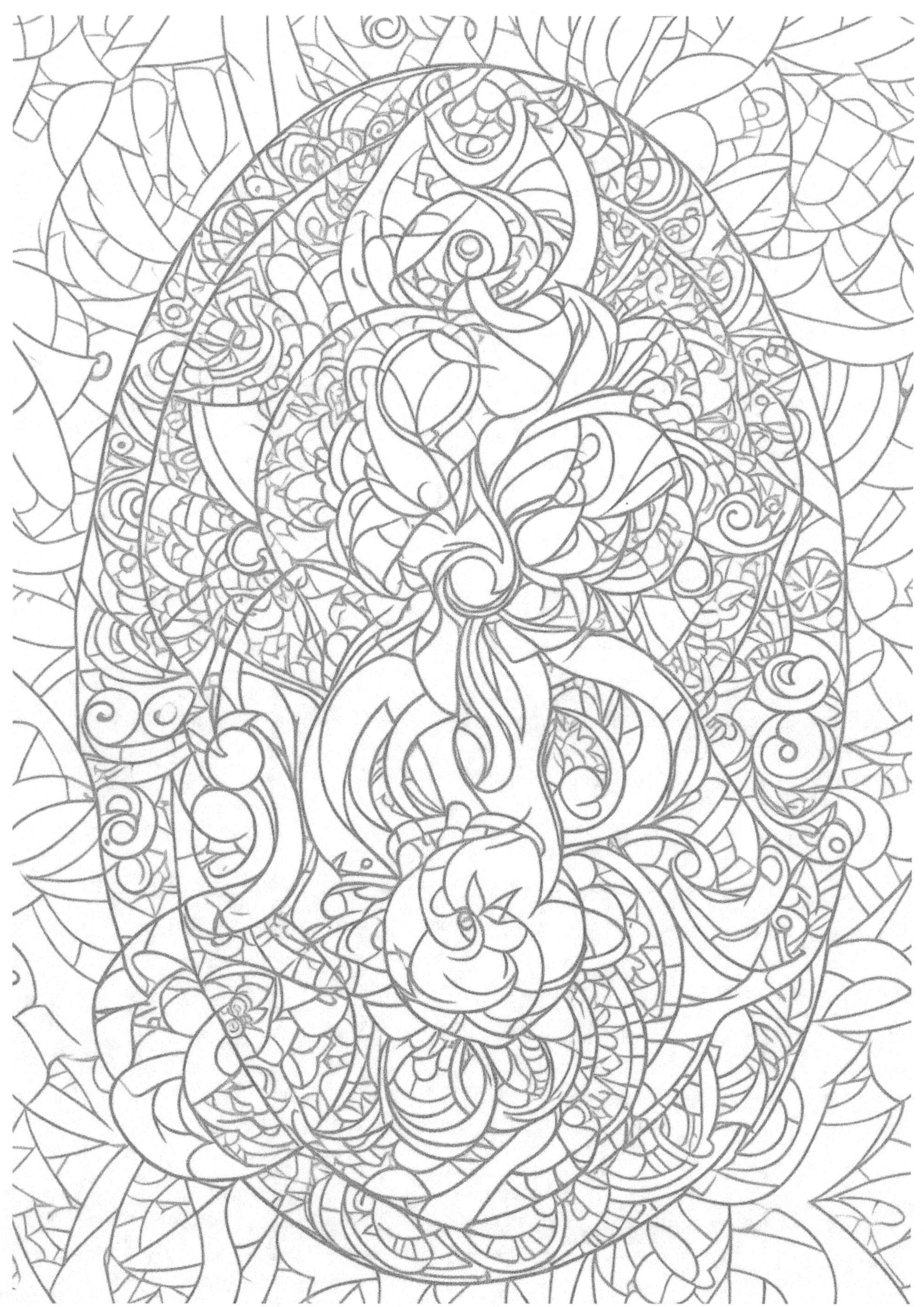

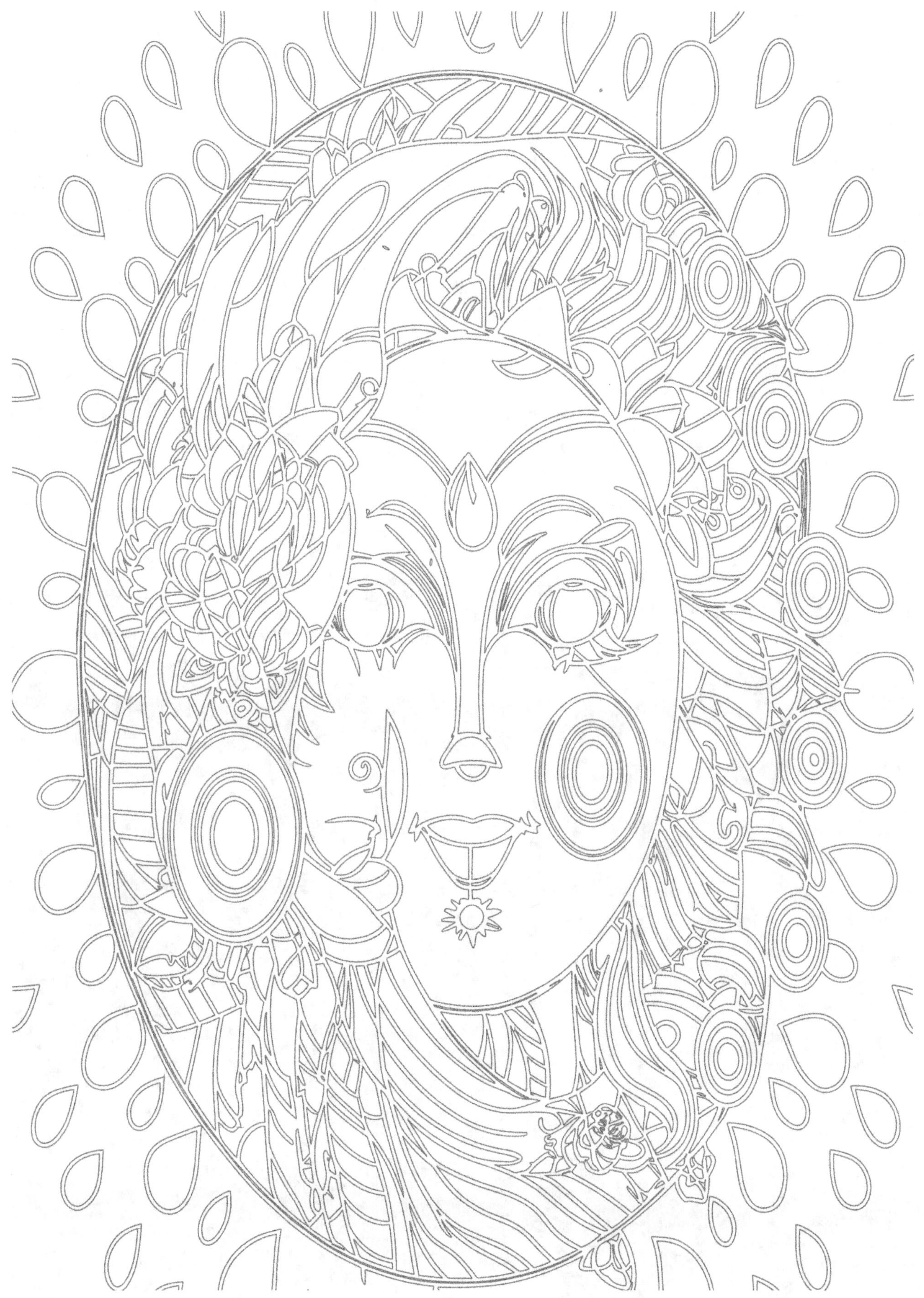

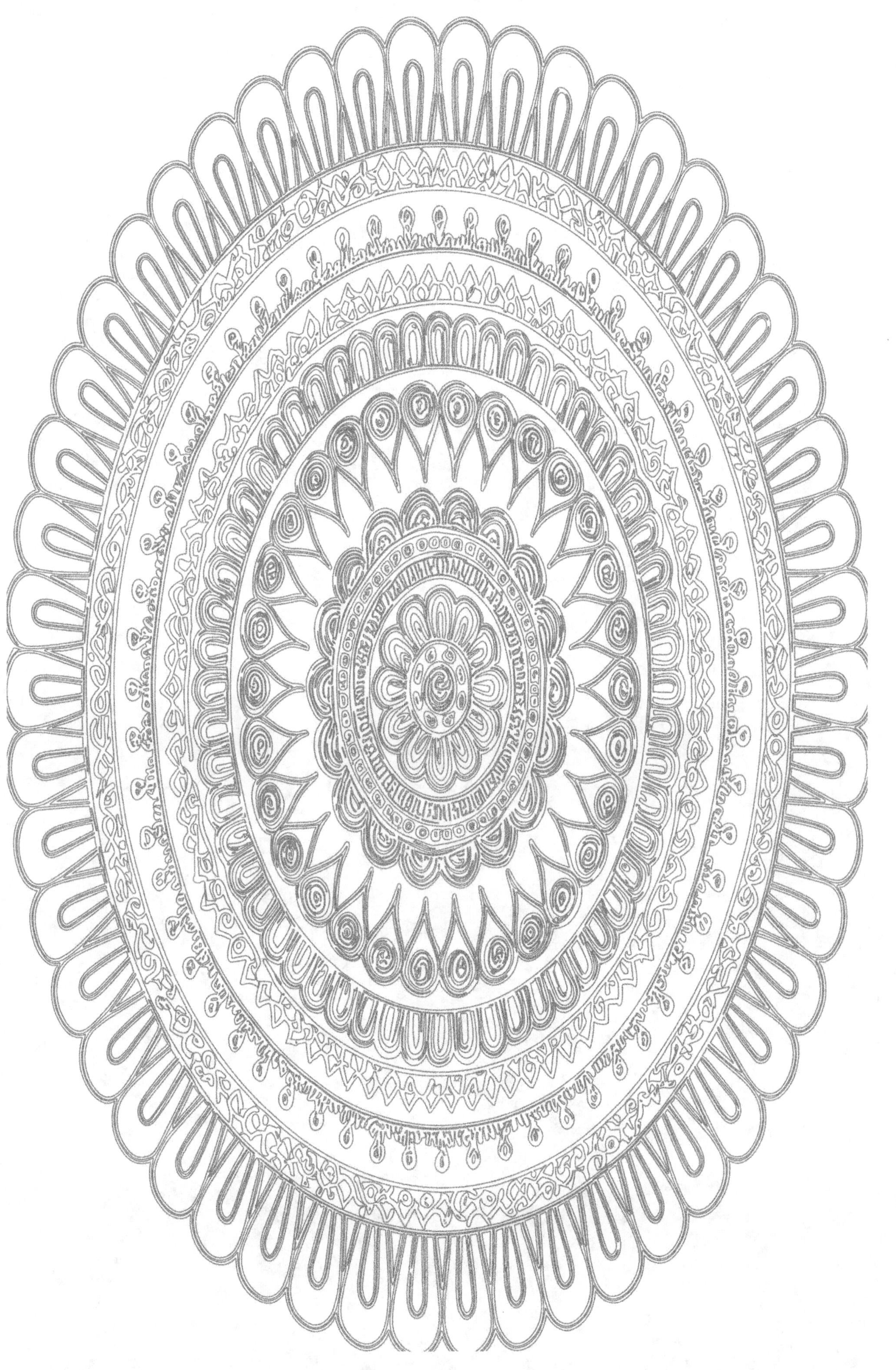

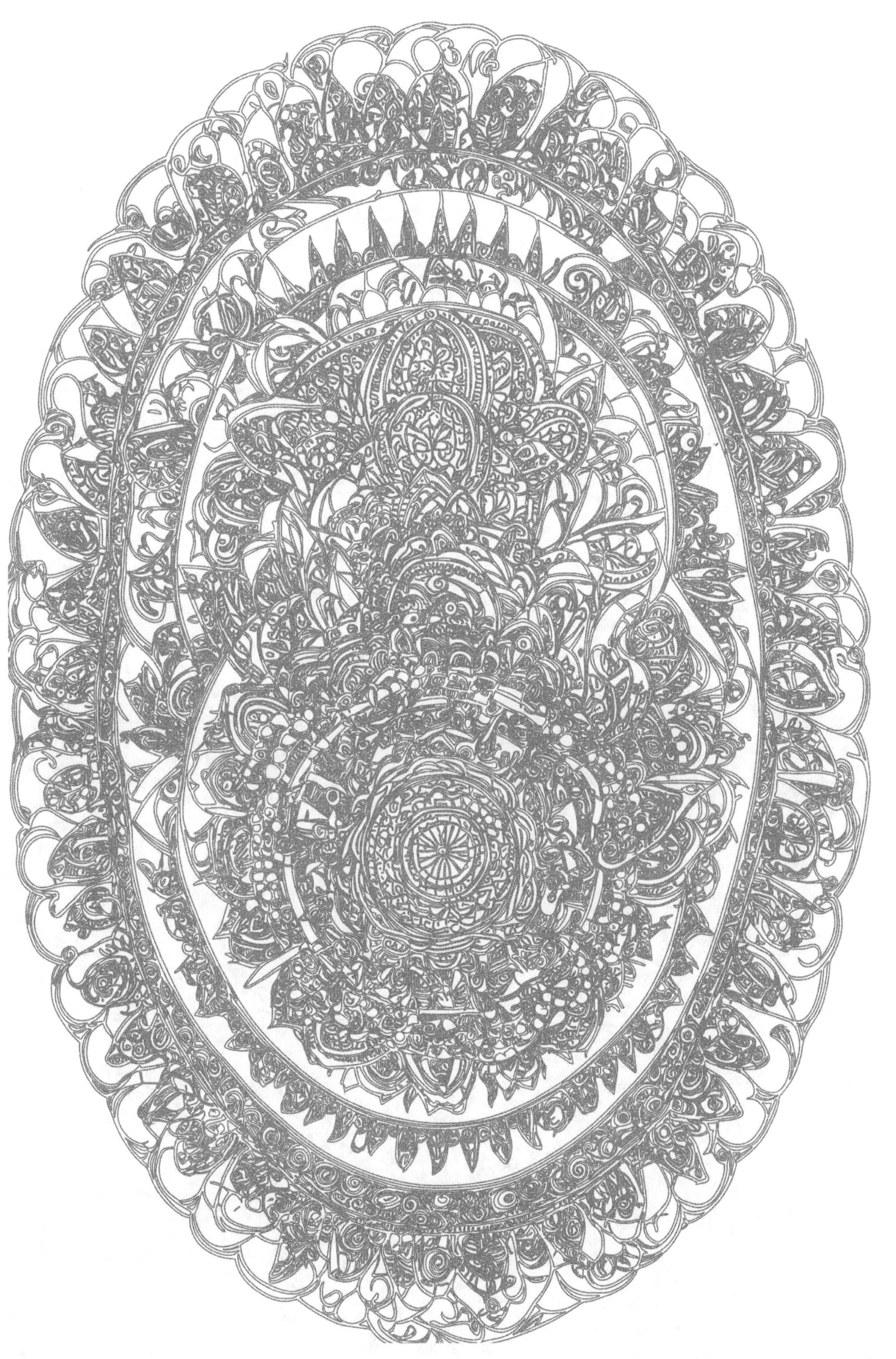

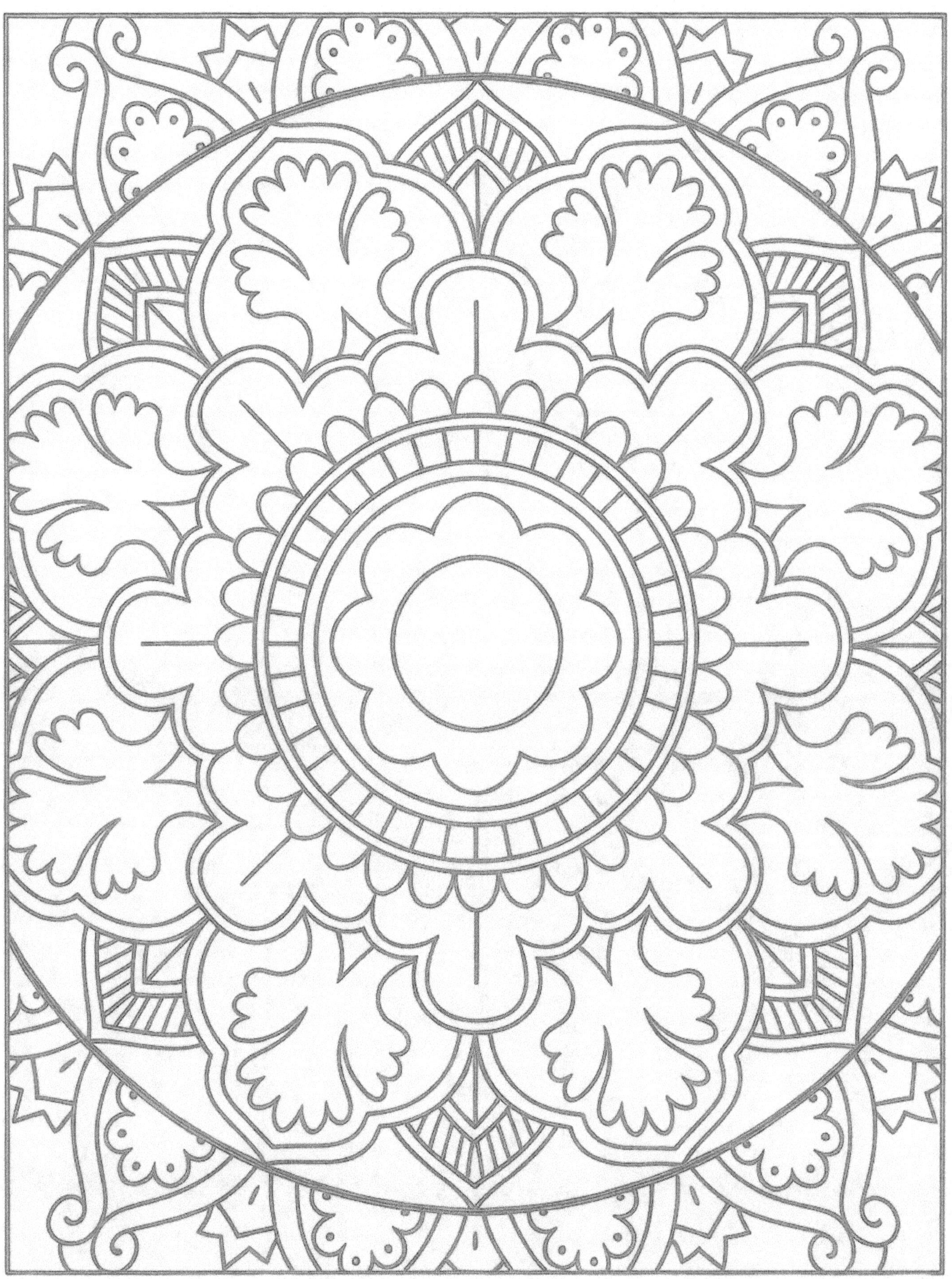

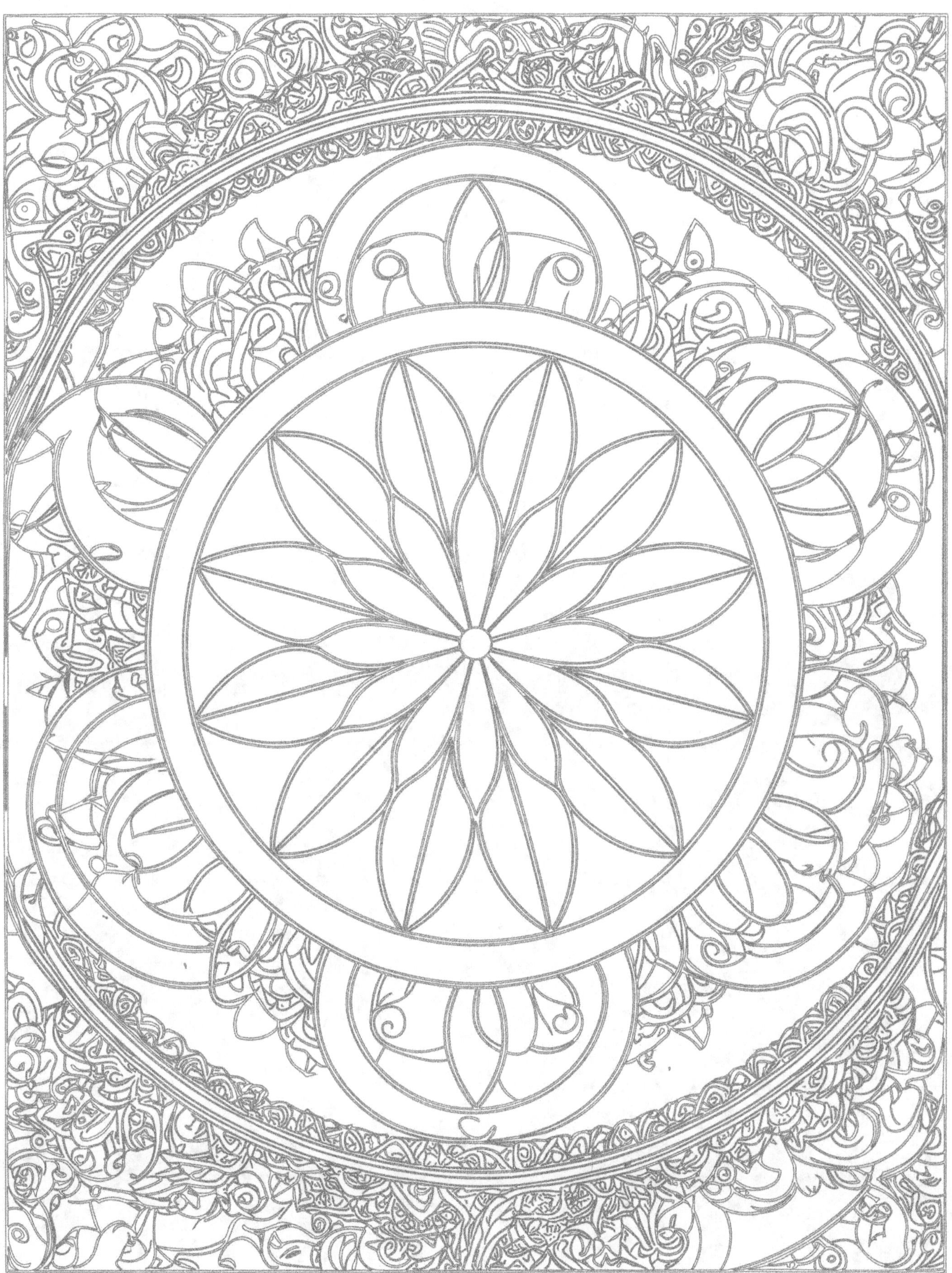

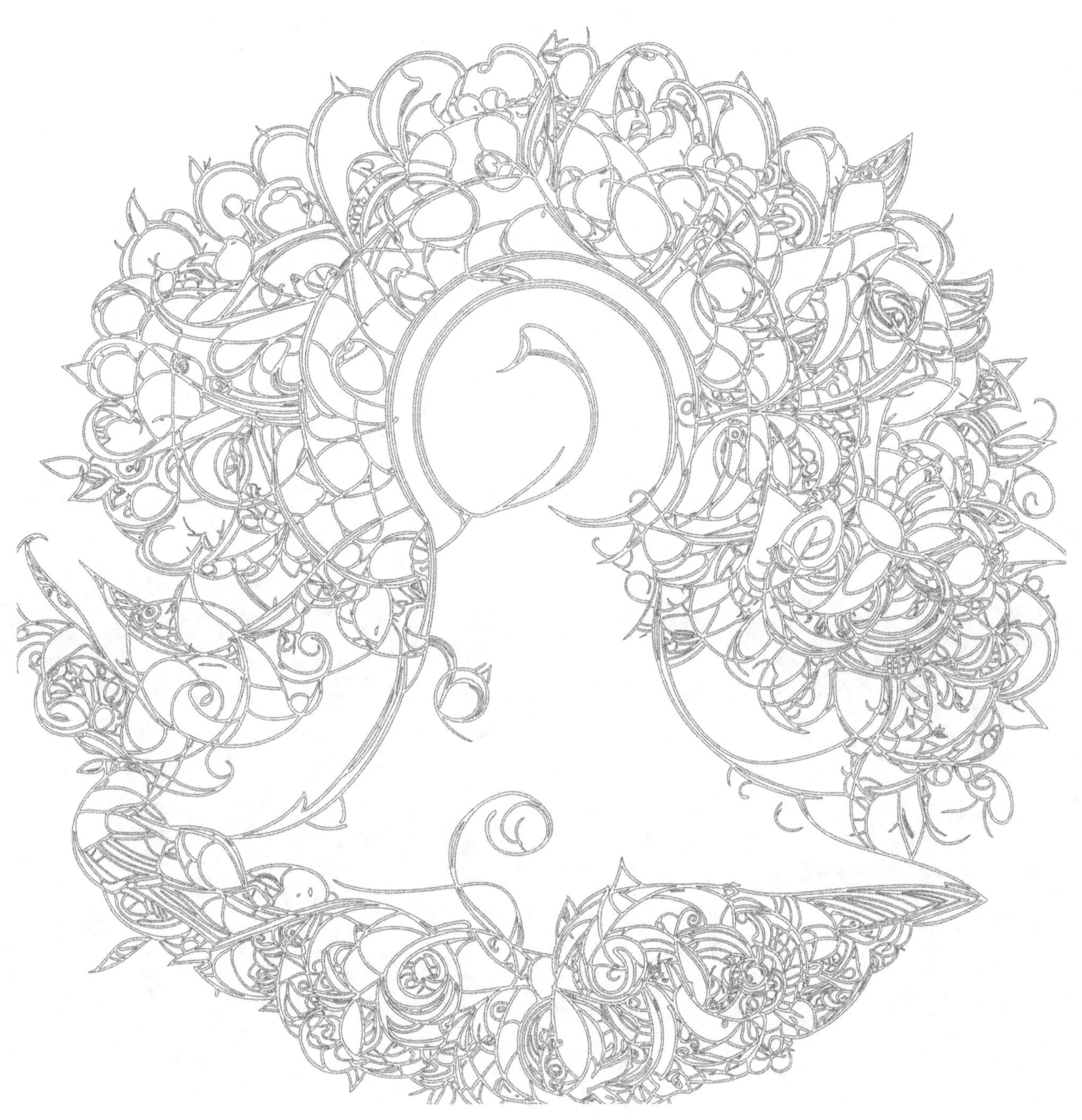

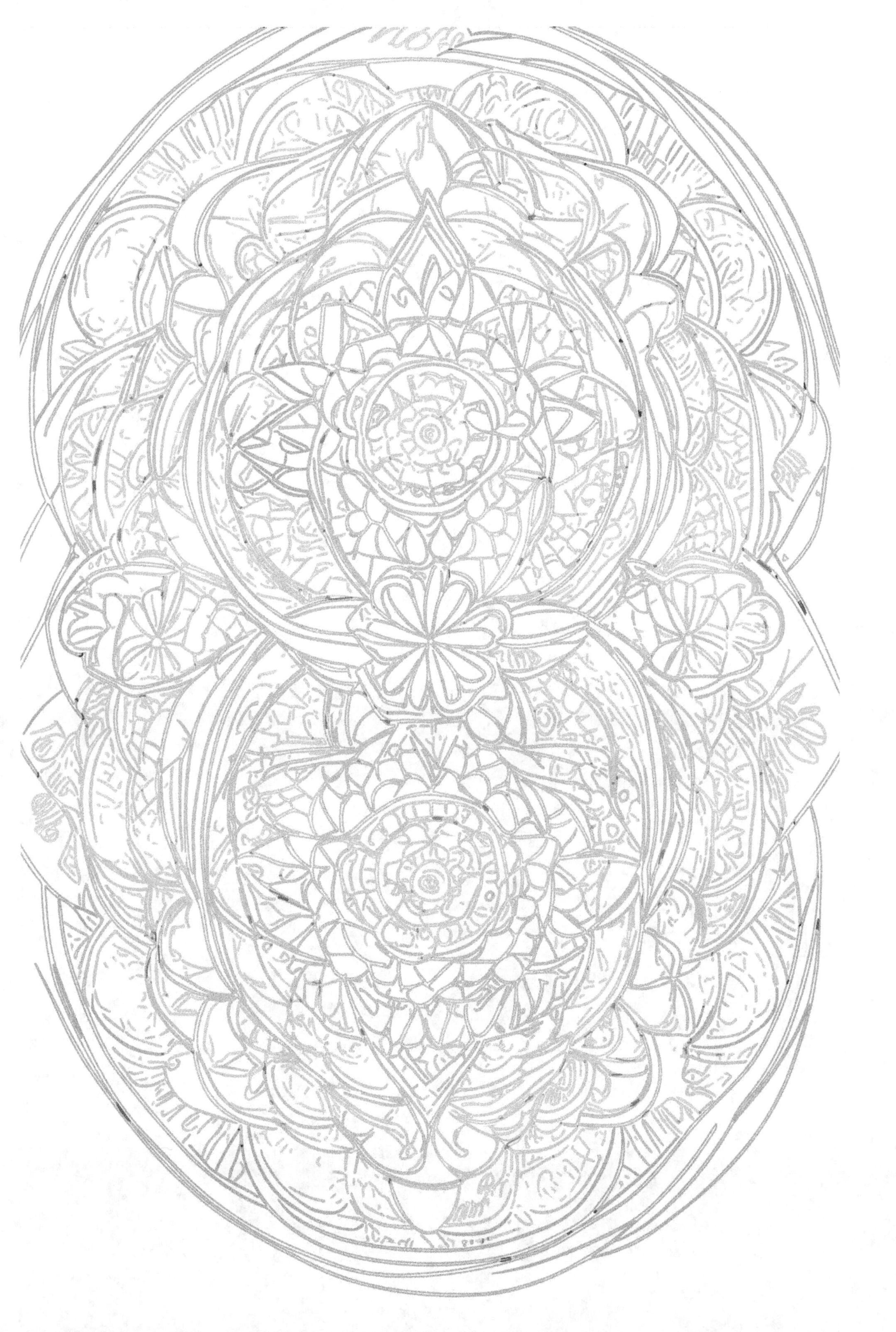

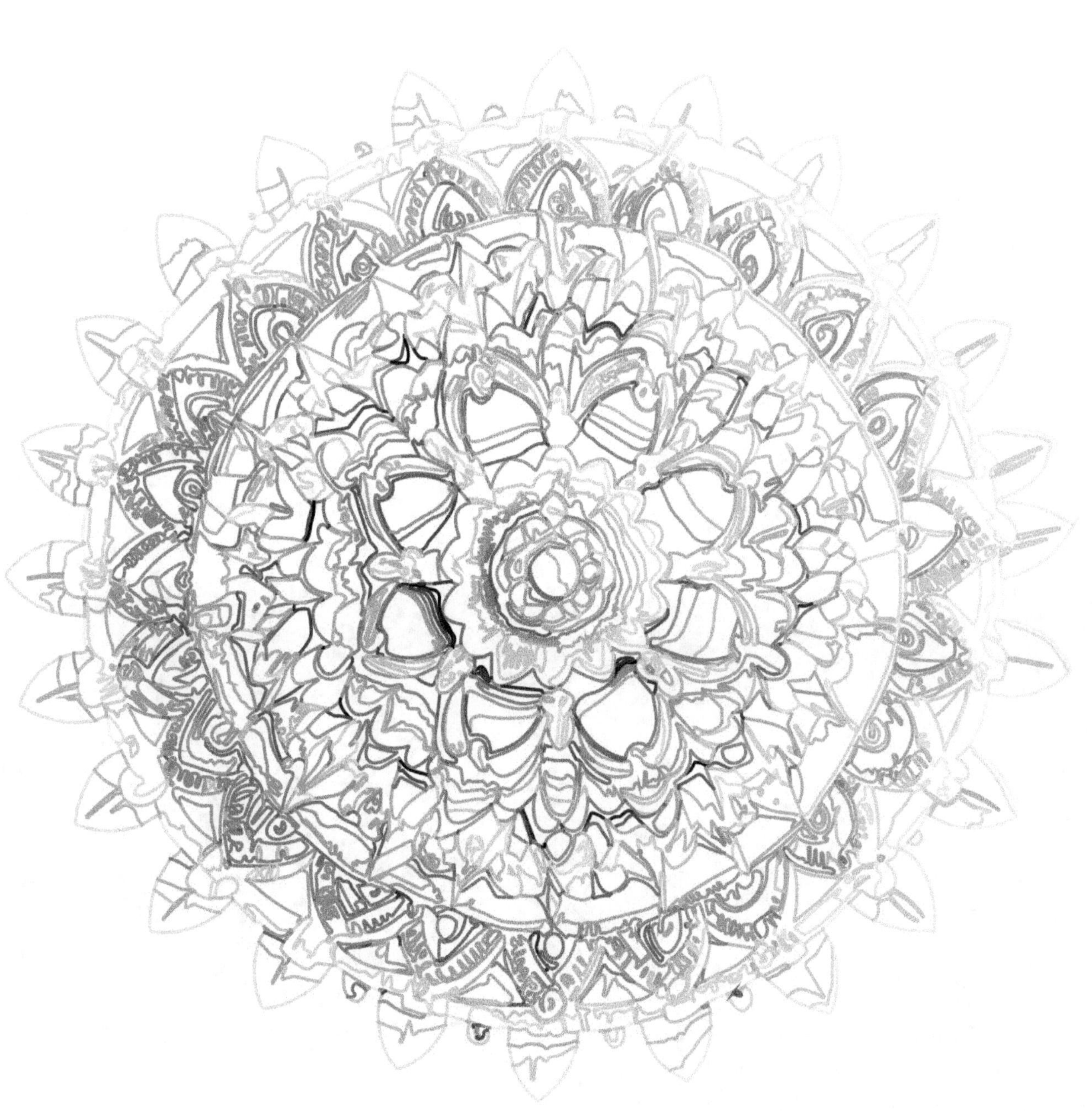

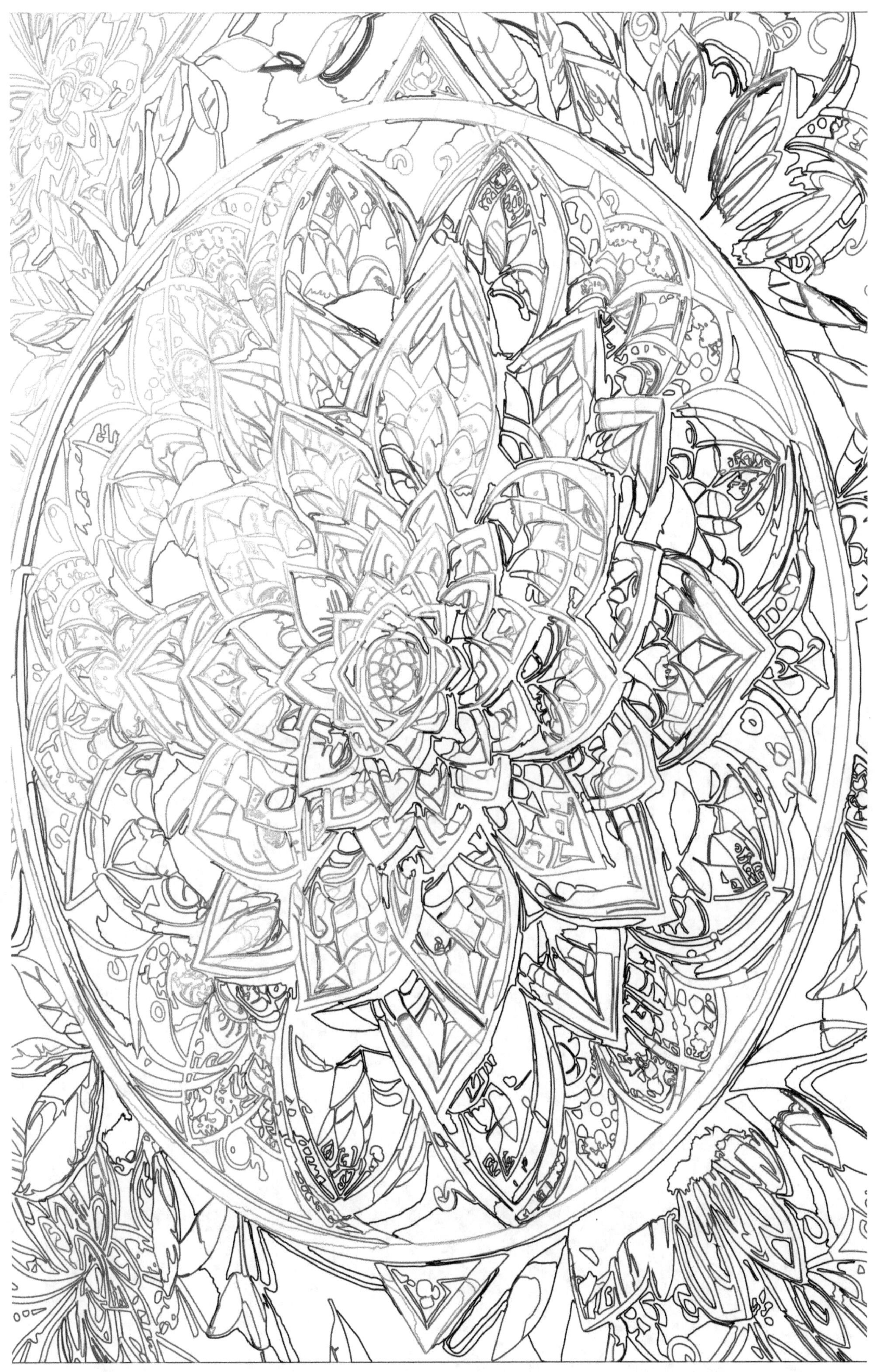

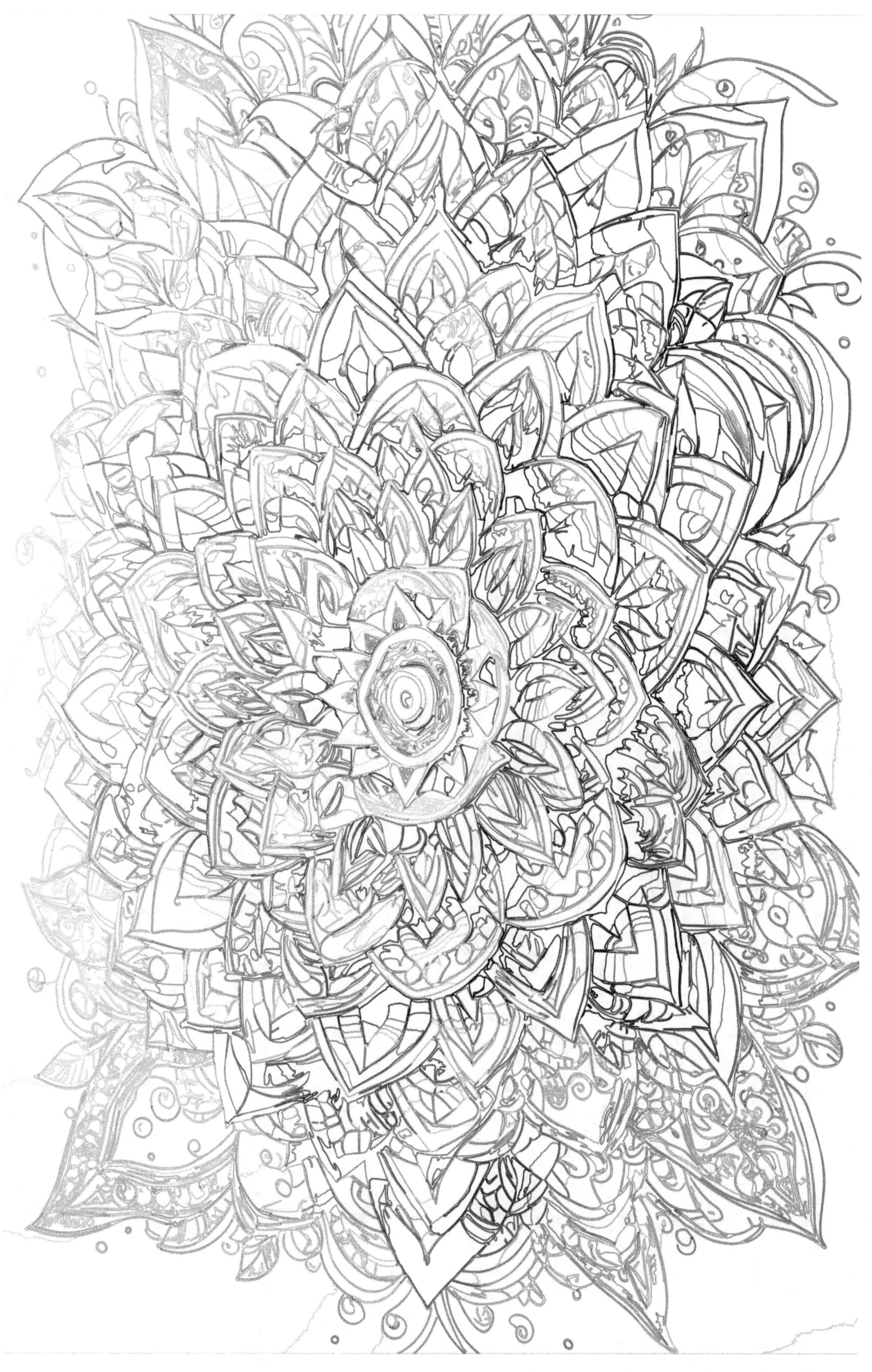

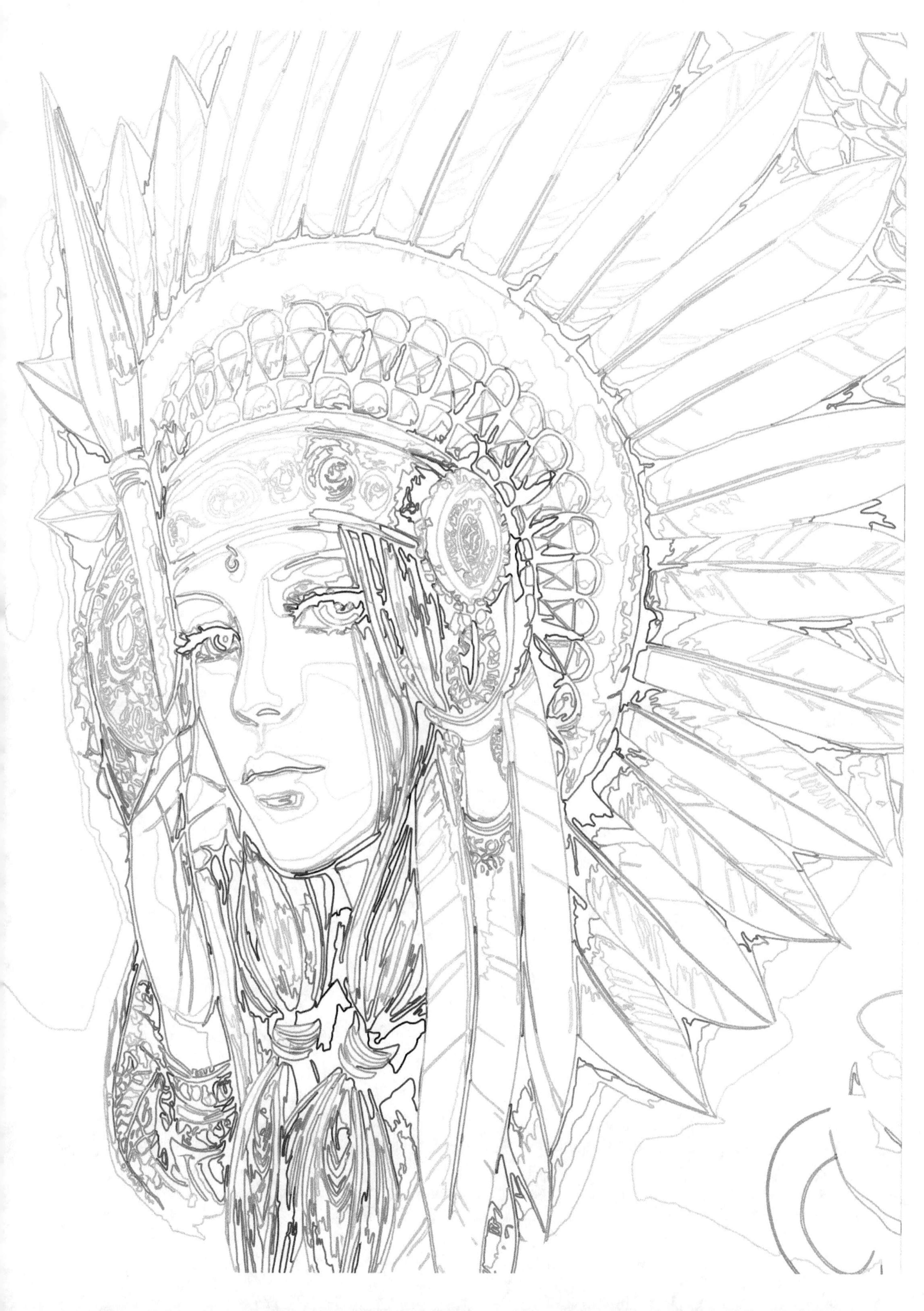

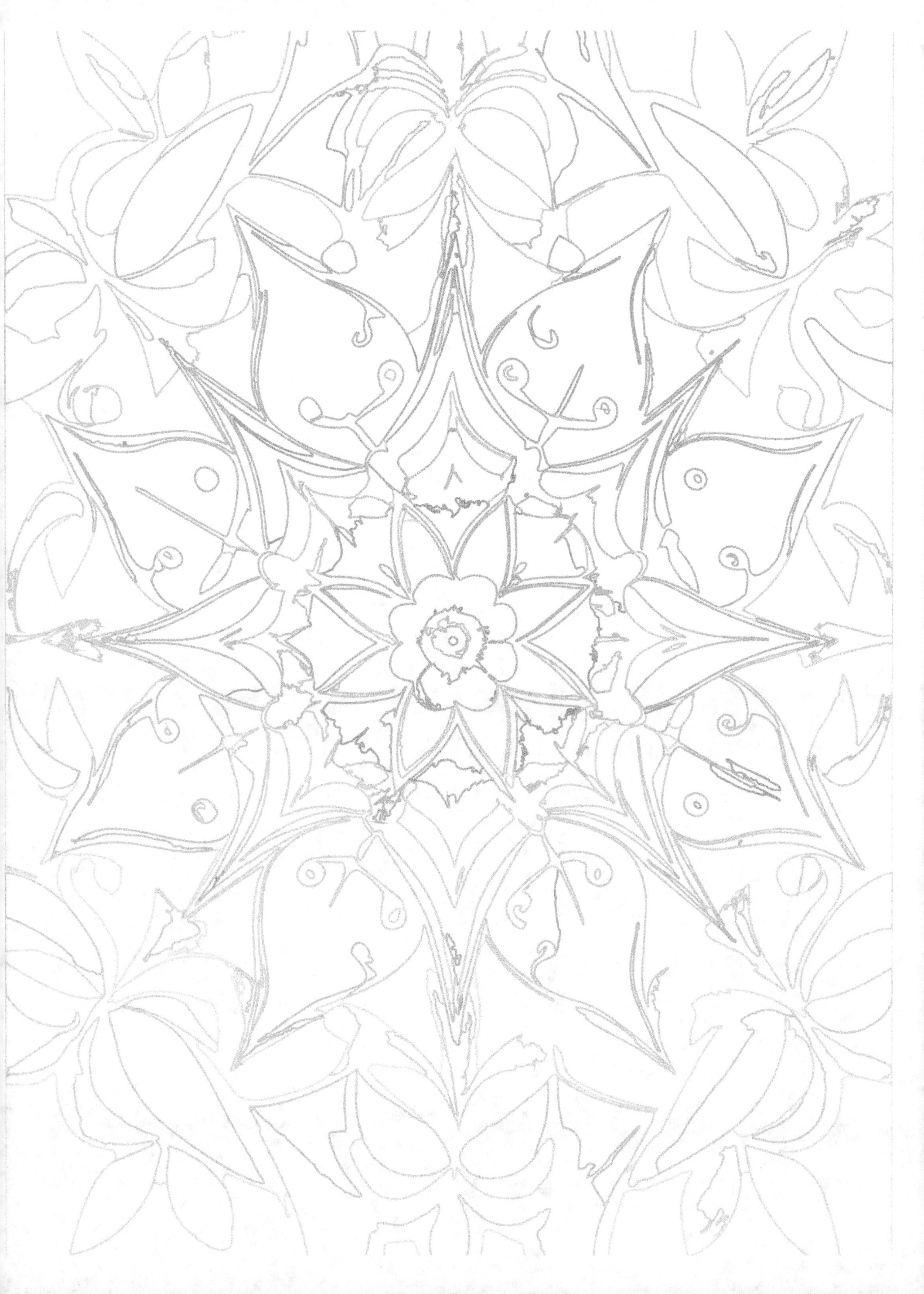

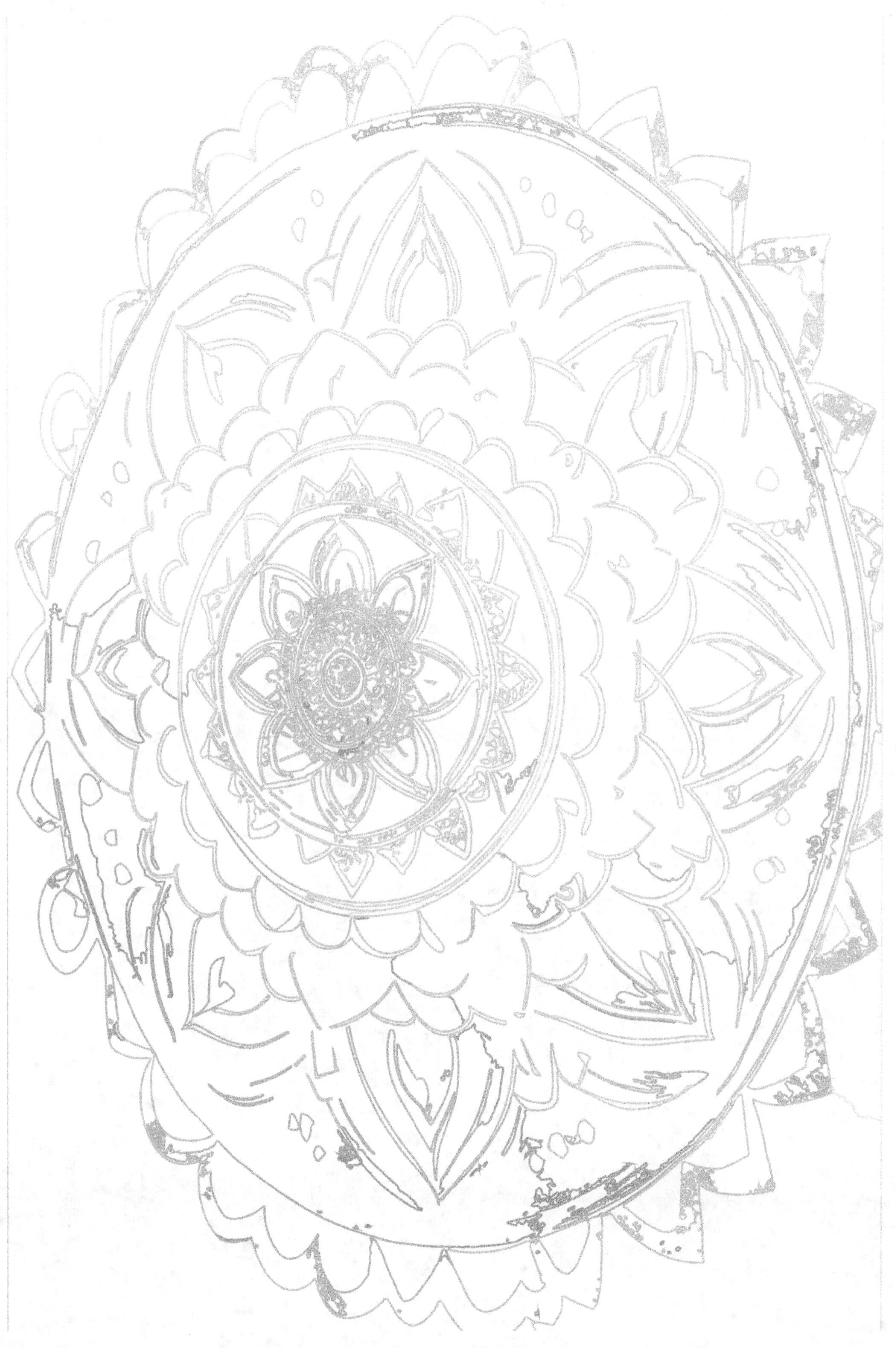

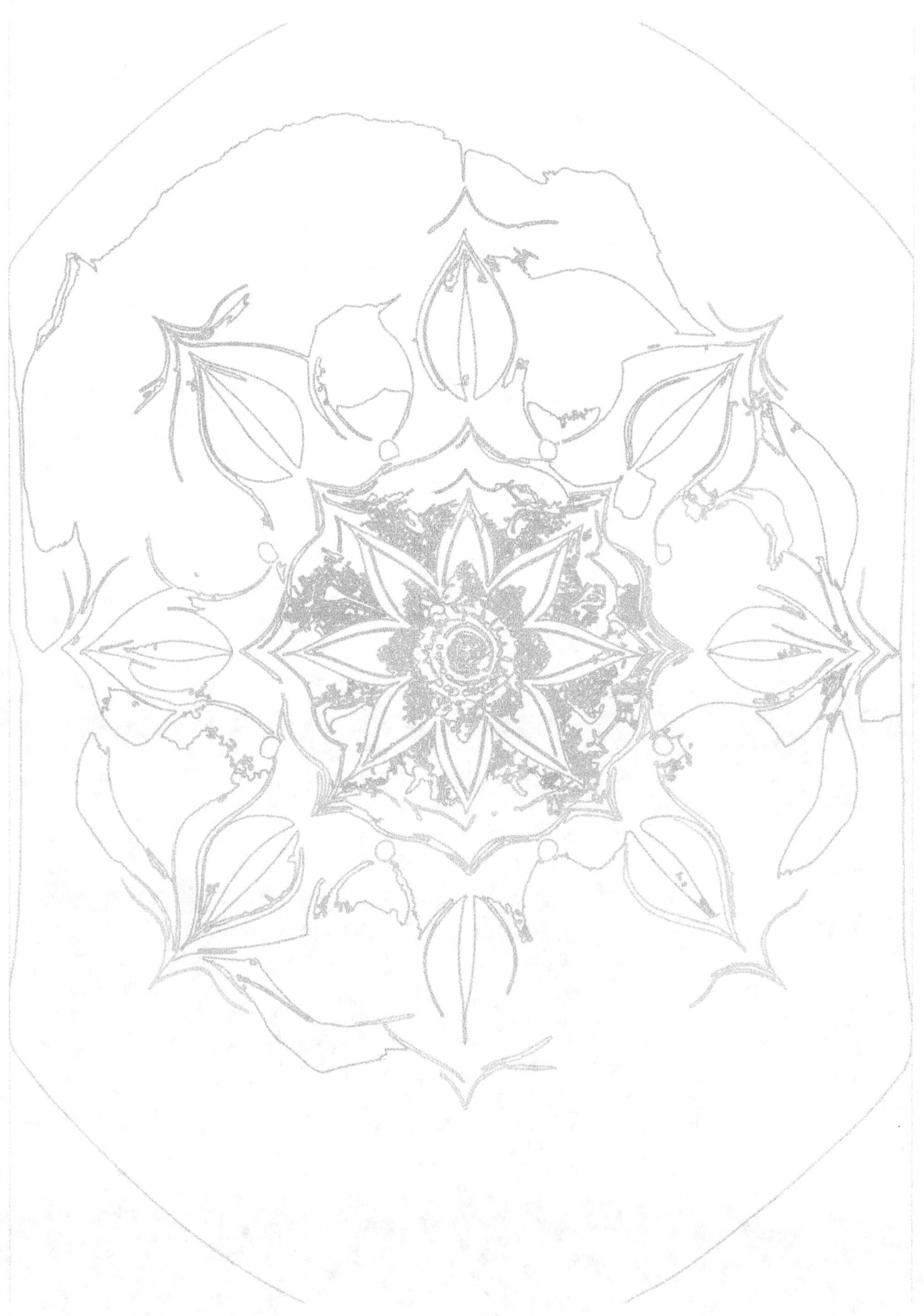

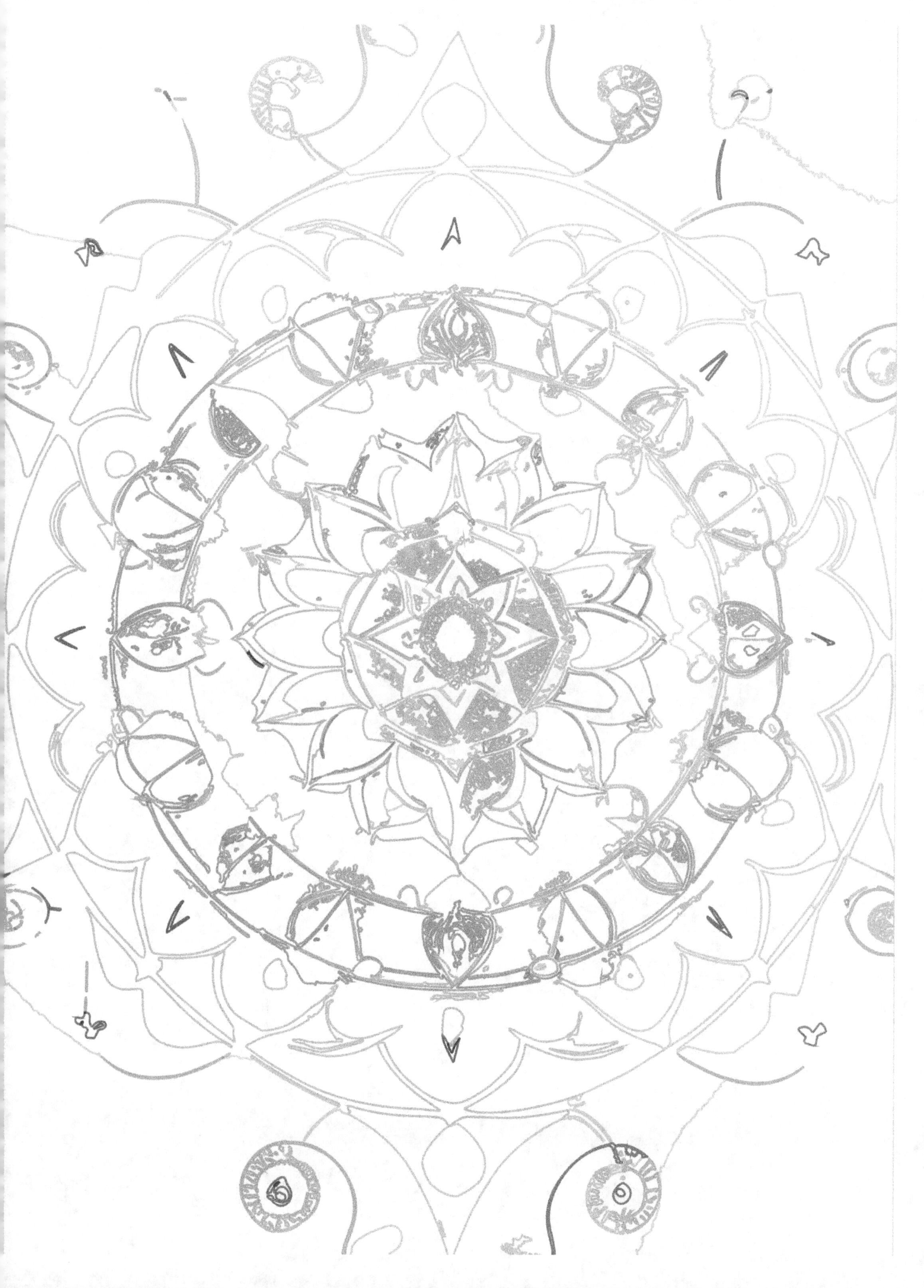

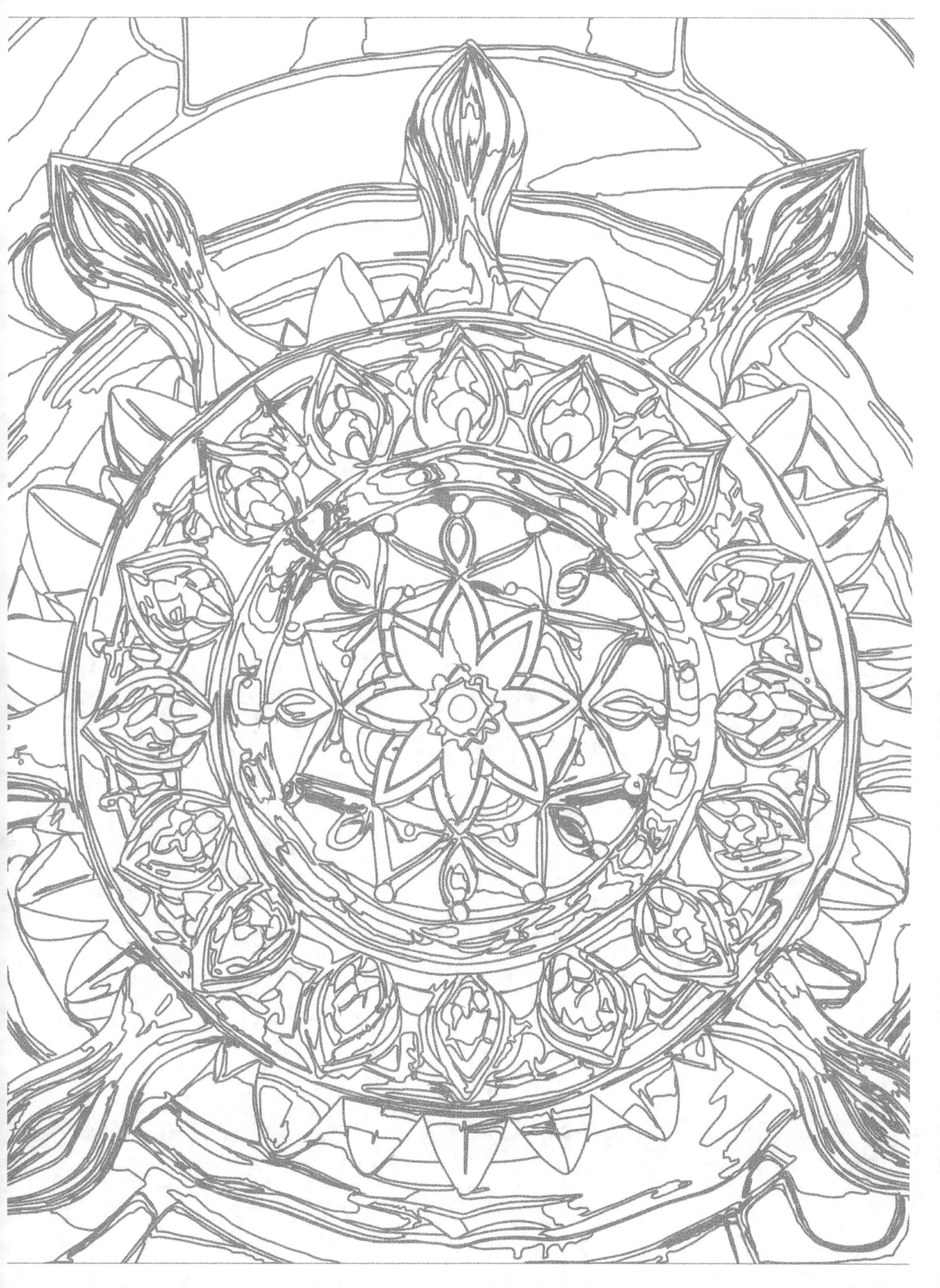

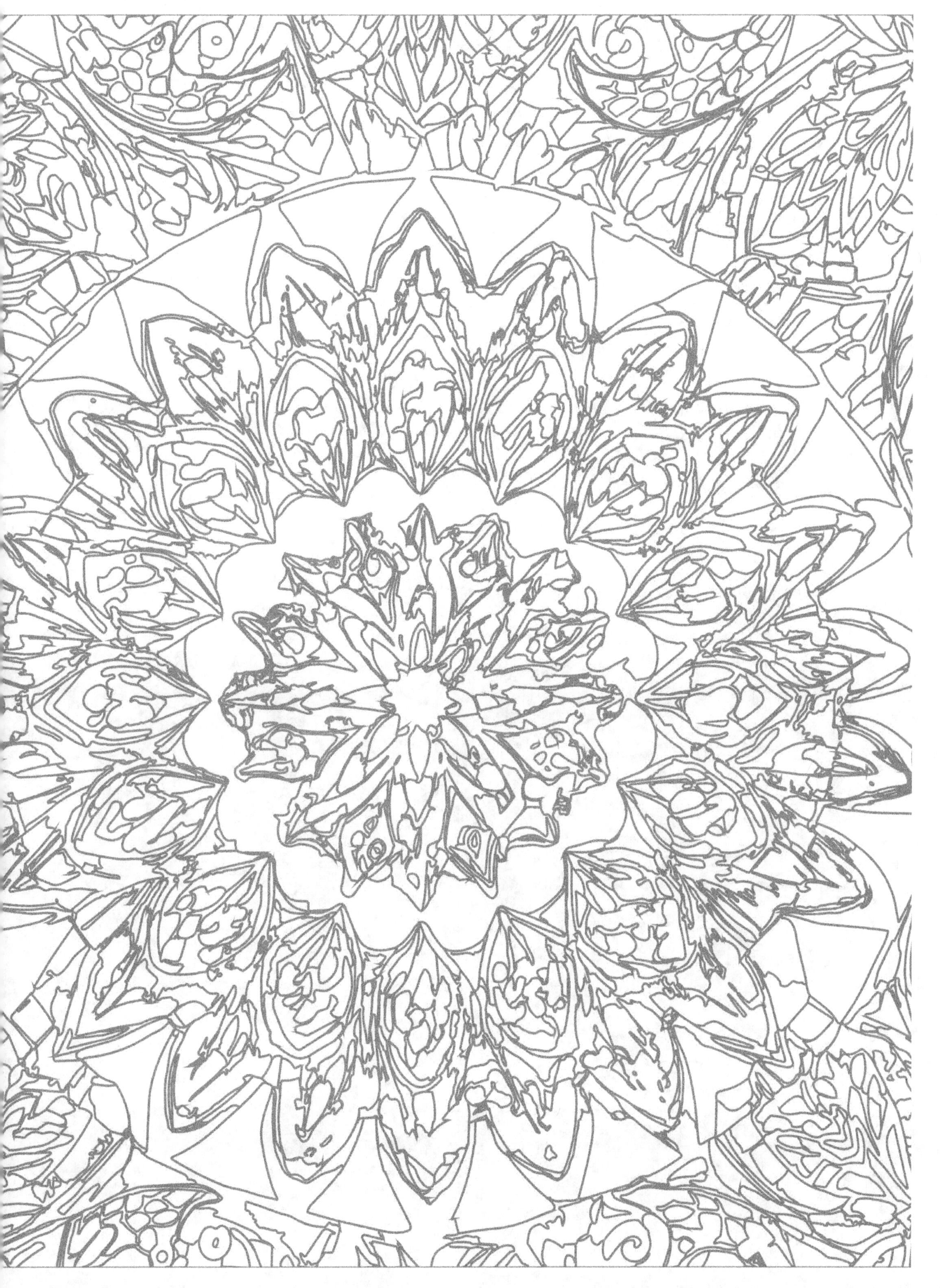